Shield The Source

Shield The Source

Brian J. Karem

NEW HORIZON PRESS
Far Hills, NJ

Copyright © 1992 by Brian Karem

All rights reserved. No part of this book may be reproduced or transmitted in any form whatsoever, including electronic, mechanical, or any information storage or retrieval system, except as may be expressly permitted by the 1976 Copyright Act or in writing from the publisher. Requests for permission should be addressed to New Horizon Press, P.O. Box 669, Far Hills, New Jersey 07931.

Library of Congress Catalog Card Number: 92-80433

Brian Karem
Shield the Source
ISBN 0-88282-104-0
New Horizon Press

"—A spot, a speck of decay, however small the limb on which it appears, and however remote it may seem from the vitals, should be alarming."
John Dickinson, 1768

Contents

Chapter 1
The Shooting — 1

Chapter 2
The Story — 12

Chapter 3
''Gang Bang'' — 30

Chapter 4
The Interview — 44

Chapter 5
Alamo Heat — 55

Chapter 6
Subpoenas — 63

Chapter 7
A Funeral — 81

Chapter 8
Searching for Evidence   87

Chapter 9
Court Battles   94

Chapter 10
Leads and Deadends   104

Chapter 11
More Questions, Few Answers   115

Chapter 12
Jail House Blues   128

Chapter 13
Dead in the Water   138

Chapter 14
Where Do We Go from Here?   163

Chapter 15
Further News   175

Chapter 16
I Won't Back Down . . .   183

Chapter 17
A Yo-Yo Existence   199

Chapter 18
Six Months in the Hole   216

Contents ix

Chapter 19
Buzzard's Luck . . . 228

Chapter 20
Sodomy No! 233

Chapter 21
Now What? 248

Chapter 22
Who Hustled This Whole Deal? 255

Chapter 23
Imprisonment Without Trial 267

Afterword 277

Acknowledgements

For Pam and Zachary, who never flinched.
For my mother, father and my grandparents.
Most especially the late Judge Fred J. Karem.
You taught me to stick by my guns.

Author's Note

These are my true experiences. The personalities, events, actions and conversations portrayed within the story have been reconstructed from extensive interviews and research, utilizing court documents, letters, personal papers, press accounts and the memories of participants. In an effort to safeguard the privacy of certain individuals, I have changed their names and, in some cases, altered otherwise identifying characteristics. Events involving the characters happened as described: only minor details have been altered.

Chapter 1

The Shooting

It was very early Monday, March 27th, 1989. Dark and cool. Henry Hernandez looked over at his older brother Julian through drunken, angry eyes as he drove through the sparse, predawn San Antonio traffic.

Henry was drunk from the tequila he'd enjoyed at a family party earlier. He was angry because, despite the hour, he still wanted to party.

The brothers had spent most of Easter Sunday celebrating at a huge family party. The weather was amiable for San Antonio. The company was excellent, the barbecue was delicious, and the liquor flowed freely.

Most of the people who had been at the party had long since gone to bed weary, but happy.

Henry, however, was not happy.

He flipped back his long, straight brown hair and fingered his mustache. Then he opened his mouth to speak and the argument with his brother continued.

Julian had most definitely lost interest in partying. And as the twenty-seven-year-old lean, dark-haired man watched Henry drive the white, monstrous Mercury Marquis down San Antonio's beltway,

IH-410, Julian let his twenty-five year old younger brother know how he felt.

The argument continued to escalate when Henry, in his heavily intoxicated condition, decided that if Julian didn't like his driving, then he could get out.

Julian, though he could be swayed by his brother's authority, had no desire to commit suicide. He knew to continue to ride with Henry would be just that. But to get out of the car would be folly, too. Henry simply shouldn't be driving.

Julian knew his little brother was beyond reasoning. Henry had no driver's license, had had too much to drink, and could barely keep the car on the road as they shouted at each other. Clearly, something had to be done.

"*I want* to drive!"

"You're too drunk," Julian told him.

"Fuck you," came Henry's reply.

Henry had enough. He saw the Broadway exit and pulled off. Up ahead was an old abandoned Burger Boy restaurant on the access road just before the Broadway intersection.

Suddenly, the lights winked on in front of a tall building near the restaurant. Henry pulled the car into the parking lot and he stopped near an automatic teller machine at what appeared to be a bank.

"Now," he shouted, "you can damn well just get out!"

"The hell I will!" Julian screamed back.

Curses flowed as the argument rose to such a feverish pitch that it could now be heard by witnesses nearly a block away.

"I'm sorry I ever got him into this," Henry would later say.

But, despite the remorse felt later, at that mo-

The Shooting

ment, the vicious screaming match came close to blows.

Then, suddenly, Henry started the car and pulled out of the building's parking lot. He was bent on spraying gravel and speeding down the access road until he could get on the highway and really open up the throttle.

But, once again, he saw the abandoned Burger Boy and the empty park bench on its lot. Henry pulled his Marquis off the access road a second time and then into the Burger Boy parking lot.

"Why couldn't we stop that fighting?" Henry later said to a local television reporter. "Nothing would have happened if we'd just stopped."

However, the fighting didn't stop.

Sixty-four-year-old Richard Barnes paced the ninth floor of the Alamo Savings Building on the northeast side of San Antonio as the Wells Fargo security guard walked his rounds. The bank was comfortably quiet. It was just before three A.M. Barnes liked to watch the twinkling of lights in the expansive city, and the view was spectacular through the massive glass windows of the office. Suddenly, as the timers kicked in, the lights came on in the parking lot about one hundred feet below him.

"It must be three," he thought to himself.

Suddenly he heard loud cursing. It sounded like it was coming from the street.

"It could be from the Pulse machine," he told himself. Criminals had harassed customers at the automated teller machine before. A dark, cool, moonless night like this was a perfect setting for those with larceny in their hearts and a knife or gun in their hands.

* * *

Henry and Julian were still parked near the park bench in the vacant Burger Boy lot.

"You're drunk. You've had enough. Hey vato, it's late Chingado!" Julian shouted.

"Fuck you." Henry was equally pissed.

"Go on, Chingado. You gonna drink forever or what?"

Julian stormed out of the car. Henry watched as Julian sat down on the park bench.

"Andele Carbone. Sonovabitch!" Julian was still very angry. He looked up from the bench, saw that Henry was still parked in the lot, so he began to walk away. Maybe Henry would leave.

Instead, Henry drove the car slowly behind his brother. Julian's tattered T-shirt blew softly in the light breeze.

Then in a burst of anger, Henry made a decision. He floored the car. His tires squealed as he drove off toward the city's west side and home. Soon, however, his hot temper began ebbing. He got back on the highway, deciding to go back and get Julian before he got into real trouble.

It was already too late.

Richard Barnes couldn't see the automated teller from his ninth floor perch. An overhang obstructed his view. So, he took the elevator down to the ground floor and walked out through the glass double doors.

When he got outside, it took a moment for his eyes to adjust. He noticed the big, cream-colored car in the bank parking lot and tried to get a closer look, but he couldn't tell what kind of car it was.

When the car pulled into the Burger Boy lot next door, Barnes figured he was watching someone trying to break into the abandoned building. Barnes went back to his office to call the police. The Alamo City

The Shooting

might be plagued with burglars, but perhaps the police would catch this pair. He dialed dutifully.

It was 3:05 A.M.

Patrol Officer Gary Williams got the call from his dispatcher at 3:07 A.M. As luck, or fate, or coincidence would have it, he was within a block of his destination and made it there within the minute.

He knew the place well. The Burger Boy was an old fast-food restaurant wedged in-between the Alamo Savings Building and another office building along the access road off of IH-410 in the city's upper-middle class northeast side. The building, which had been vacant for months, was made of brick and trimmed in orange plastic. It seemed out of place; a carcass of a fast-food haven near no other.

Gary looked at the restaurant and prided himself on how well he knew his district. Gary was in his thirties, a Vietnam veteran, and considerably older than most recruits when he joined the force. But he had passed the San Antonio Police Department's rigorous entrance exam and survived life as a cadet to become a police officer. On arduous physical assignments, he hung in there with the youngest officers and he enjoyed the reputation of a tough, no-nonsense cop who did his job. His superiors said the younger officers looked up to Gary and often sought out his opinions and advice, believing them sound and level-headed.

Gary was thorough in his reports and in all other police matters. He was punctual and friendly. But most of his coworkers on the dog-watch shift at the city's northeast police substation did not think of Gary as a close friend.

In fact, many of his coworkers thought of Gary as a loner—a man who kept to himself off the job, but seemed responsible, reasonable, and mature on the job. Some of Gary's superiors attributed his solitude and insight to his age. Since he was so much older than the other rookies when he joined the force, he had experienced more of life than the younger cops. A lot of the men at Gary's precinct just thought Gary didn't have much in common with the younger guys.

Others, like his fellow officer Cris Anders, who was closer to Gary than most, thought he was a quiet, likeable guy who put in his hours and went home. When Gary's divorce problems began brewing, most of the men on the force who thought they knew Gary couldn't believe he was to blame for any of the problems.

Yet, there may have been another side to Williams that not many got to see. Perhaps his wife did, and that was reflected in the divorce papers. Perhaps others had seen it as well.

Less than a week ago, he'd been accused of beating a prisoner with a flashlight. The San Antonio police call it "tuning up" a prisoner. It's an accomplished art form required for survival on the streets. A "tune up" may result when an officer must fight for his life, or it could come from reasons much darker.

Gary pulled his patrol car into the restaurant's lot.

"3302," Williams said, using his call numbers. "I'm 10-6."

Williams was at the scene. He hadn't called for a backup. Later it would be said that he routinely waved off backup officers on his calls, and that he often stayed out of touch with his dispatcher.

Barnes saw Williams pull into the darkened lot with his police light off. It was standard procedure. Better to catch the burglars in the act than blaring the

The Shooting

lights, sounding the siren, and possibly scaring them off.

At the abandoned building, Williams aimed the large "sun gun" light, which was mounted on the patrol car's frame just outside the driver's side window. With the aid of the powerful light, he could see through the building's full-length plate glass windows. It looked dingy, dusty, and abandoned. As he continued to pass the light back and forth, he could see evidence of tampering or a break-in. The building had been abandoned for months. What would burglars want here anyway?

Gary drove around the building and found nothing out of the ordinary in the back. He continued his surveillance and headed his car back to the front of the building.

Then, Gary saw Julian.

A Hispanic man in his twenties wearing a T-shirt and jeans, walking near an abandoned building raised all of Gary's warning flags.

What was the guy doing out at this hour? His clothing was none too fancy. Was he a drug addict? Did he try to break-in? Where was he going now? Was he drunk?

Williams flipped on his emergency lights. Gary Williams was about to stop and investigate what the police call "a suspicious person."

Just then Henry pulled back into the lot. With most of his anger gone, and the fatigue brought on by the lateness of the hour biting at him, all he wanted to do was get Julian and go home. He couldn't leave his brother here on the city's northeast side no matter what they had been arguing about. It wasn't right.

The Anglos at that end of town would blame a Hispanic for anything. The westside was for vatos. Everyone knew that. If Henry didn't pick up Julian, his brother could get into all kinds of trouble.

Barnes, from his position just outside the Alamo Savings Building, watched the cream-colored car cruising west on the access road. That surprised him. He thought the car was still on the Burger Boy lot. It must have left while he had called the cops. As the car pulled into the Burger Boy lot, he noticed a man walking toward the car. Then the emergency lights came on in the police cruiser.

Williams, noting that Henry had pulled up, typed the license number of the Mercury into his mobile police computer inside his cruiser. A few short seconds later, Gary Williams got out of his patrol car. He now had two "suspicious persons" to investigate and perhaps a car to search.

Gary got to Henry's car just as Julian got inside.

Right away, Henry felt that the cop had "some kind of attitude." "He acted like he just wanted to grab someone," Henry said later.

Williams' first act was to demand identification from both men.

"Let's see your license," he said.

Henry didn't have one.

"Okay, out of the car," demanded Williams.

Henry knew what was coming. He was no stranger to cops or jail.

"Hey man, take it easy!" Henry thought the cop was being more than a little rough.

"I'll take it easy, come on!" Williams yanked him by both arms and forced him toward the patrol car.

Julian looked over and saw his brother yelling at the cop.

"Stop it, Henry!" he shouted. Then he looked at the cop. "Hey, don't pay any attention to him. He's drunk."

The Shooting

Williams was in no mood to mess with two drunks. They had no respect for the law. No respect for him. He reached out and grabbed Henry again. This time he struck Henry with his police flashlight.

"Fuck you," Henry said.

Julian saw the cop swinging at his brother with a large, black metal flashlight. "Hey, leave my brother alone!" Julian tried to reach out and keep the cop from hitting Henry again.

Williams bit his lip, overcome with how quickly things were getting out of hand. These two bastards had the nerve to fight him! He struck the one with the black hair as he came out of the car after him—even as he continued to struggle with the smart-mouthed one with brown hair who'd been driving. Williams realized he needed his gun to stop this.

From the ground, Julian saw the officer reach for his police issued, chrome plated .357 magnum.

"Henry, watch out! He's got a gun! Este vato tiene una pistola! Cuidado!"

"You son of a bitch!" Henry shouted as he struggled to keep the tall, stocky officer from shooting him. He clawed and fought. As a last resort, he reached up and bit the officer's neck as Williams struck him again.

"You son of a bitch," Henry shouted. Henry, small, wiry and drunk, struggled to keep the stocky, taller officer from shooting him. He clawed and fought as if his life depended on it. As a last resort, he reached up and bit the officer's neck as hard as he could even as the officer struck him again.

Julian again looked at the revolver. The light from the street lamps glistened off the gun as both Henry and the officer struggled for control. Suddenly, it was up in the air. A loud flash. An explosion rocked the night air.

* * *

Henry Wills, a fifty-two year old news carrier for the *San Antonio Express-News* heard the gunshot as he was driving underneath the Broadway overpass at 410. He brought his car to a quick stop, turned it around in the parking lot of the Sizzler Steak House, and headed back to where he thought he had heard the shot.

Barnes, meanwhile, watched the scene from a distance near the automatic teller in front of Alamo Savings. He thought he saw Williams walk to the trunk of the cream-colored car and then talk to a man at the vehicle.

Then he heard, "Son of a bitch!" and a loud gun shot. What the hell was going on?

Officer Williams wondered the same thing. The force of the blast stunned him and knocked him on the ground. Then he felt the pain in his neck. He was bleeding. Not from a gunshot wound, but the son of a bitch had bit him! He clenched his fists.

Henry and Julian both saw the anger in the officer's eyes as he struggled to his feet.

"Hey. Hey let's forget it. Let's forget about it," Julian was pleading.

"Yeah," Henry said, standing over the officer with the .357 in his hand. "Let's forget it."

Williams was having none of it. He rushed Henry grabbing for the gun. They fought hard. Williams knew his only hope of regaining control of the situation was to get his revolver back. He lunged for it, but the slippery little shit was strong and wiry.

As they fought, Henry mustered every ounce of strength he could to keep from giving up the gun. There was no reasoning with anyone now. This was a matter of survival.

Then Williams got hold of the gun barrel. They struggled and suddenly fell away from each other. An-

The Shooting   11

other shot exploded in the darkness. This time Williams hit the ground and didn't get up.

"Shit, he's shot, he's shot!" Julian shouted.

"You can go now. You can go now," Williams said. It seemed to make no sense.

Suddenly it was Henry who came to his senses. "What's a matter with you, man? Let's get the fuck out of here!"

The brothers scrambled for their car with Henry still clasping the police revolver in his hand. They sped out of the parking lot, Julian driving the wrong way down the road. Henry, dazed and confused, looked at the revolver again. What the hell just happened? Suddenly scared, Henry tossed the gun out of the car window.

Lying on the ground, Williams began groaning. Almost instinctively, he reached over to his radio and punched the orange emergency button which sent a signal notifying the dispatcher and the world that he was in trouble.

He struggled to speak. Finally, just after 3:19 A.M., not more than twelve minutes since he got the initial call, Williams called in to the dispatcher for the last time.

"I'm shot," he gasped.

"3302, 10-4," the dispatcher replied calmly. "First officer out, advise 3302 says he's been hit."

"They're in the car. They're . . ." Williams struggled up on an elbow trying to finish his sentence. Pain flooded in and he could only manage a long sigh, then: "They're westbound."

Chapter 2

The Story

It was now 3:30 A.M. that same Monday. The telephone rang once, twice. The third time I struggled out of bed, rubbed the sleep out of my eyes and noted the time displayed by the soft green light of the alarm clock.

Two police officers had been shot in San Antonio in the last two weeks, and since as a reporter for KMOL-TV, I cover the police beat, I'd left a standing request with the station's overnight photographer to contact me if another officer was involved in a shooting.

As I reached for the telephone, I knew instinctively this wasn't going to be good news.

On the other end of the line I heard Bill Davenport, the station's overnight spot news photographer. While the rest of us sleep, Davenport and a handful of other hearty, underpaid photographers and reporters have the unenviable task of going to all overnight news events. These stories can range from car wrecks to fires, from bad weather to craziness.

"What's up, Daffy?" I mumbled, still only half coherent.

"A cop shooting," he reported.

The beep at the end of Davenport's conversation

The Story

and the poor quality of the telephone reception told me Davenport was on the scene and calling from the station's hand-held two-way radio that also serves as a mobile telephone.

"What happened?"

"A cop got shot with his own gun while making a traffic stop."

"Did they catch the guy?"

"No, but the police know who it was. They left their driver's license."

I was confused about the plural reference to the shooter, but spit out the next question preprogrammed in my head."

"How's the cop?"

"I think he's gonna be okay. He's in the ambulance now and talking with the paramedics."

I let out a sigh of relief. It appeared the officer would live. At least, I thought, I wouldn't be covering another police fatality.

Since the bizarre drowning of Officer Patty Calderon two days after Christmas it appeared to be one mishap after another for local police. Calderon died while chasing a small-time thief who had stolen a pack of cigarettes from a convenience store. He ran down a steep, wooded embankment and jumped into the creek at the bottom of the hill. The pretty, petite Calderon, wearing boots, her gun and gun belt, as well as a bullet-proof vest, had run after the man for nearly a mile when she hit the creek. It was deeper than she was tall, and the weight of her equipment combined with the fatigue she felt from the mile-long run kept her from reaching the sanctuary of the bank, which was less than five feet from where she drowned.

Police found her body hours later. Apparently she had gotten off most of her heavy equipment—but her efforts to extricate herself were unsuccessful.

I shook off the mental image of nearly a dozen police officers in tears as they dragged the dead woman from that creek.

"I can be on my way in about five minutes, Daffy. Where are you?"

"I'm standing behind the police cars."

"I mean," I said, "Where did it happen?" Daffy, along with everyone else I've ever known in news, cannot resist a smart remark. Straight lines are not something we ignore in our newsroom.

"We're over on 410 near Broadway. You know where that abandoned Burger Boy restaurant is?"

I had a fairly good idea and promised to meet him there.

Hanging up the telephone, I pulled on my blue jeans, white shirt, red tie, and navy blue jacket. Then I hunted down the peripatetic white sneakers, combed my black hair and walked over to wake my wife.

"What is it?" Pam sleepily asked from the deep warm security of the comforter.

"Another cop got shot." I grimaced, "I'll take the car and be back as soon as possible."

She took a minute to shake herself awake. "You won't be back by the time I go to work will you?"

"I don't know."

Pam wasn't about to let me take the car; we only had one, and she had to go to work and take our two month old son, Zachary, finally asleep after a wakeful night, to the day nursery. She didn't want to get up now, but would rather do so than risk being stranded later.

As she dressed we discussed the shooting. Making these trips put her in close touch with some of the more gruesome stories I've covered. Each episode had left lasting impressions in both of our minds.

Pam bundled up the baby and we all got into the

car. I headed for Interstate 410, the city's major beltway. Later exiting at Nacogdoches I drove down the access road toward Broadway. We arrived at the scene of the shooting a few minutes later. I kissed Pam and Zack goodbye as she scooted over to the driver's side of the car. Outside, I began winding my way through a tangle of police cars to a spot where I could see a knot of reporters and cameras assembled.

Police cars had encircled the abandoned Burger Boy restaurant, and the headlights from the cars illuminated the universal yellow tape—indicator of crime scenes.

Inside the tape, several police officers from the shooting team were already going over the area. Even at the early hour of four A.M., the police officers were wearing their two-piece suits. The only noticeable difference in the sea of dark suits was Sergeant John Lopez, whose cowboy hat towered above the rest.

Lying on the ground, inside the tape, I saw what appeared to be a police bullet proof vest, a police badge, a holster, and some red stained cloth.

Off to the side Police spokesman Paul Buske, looking like a rumpled Mr. Magoo, squinted into the bright television lights. He told the reporters that the officer was "conscious and breathing," and was expected to live. Then he reported that he'd been shot twice; once in the abdomen just under his bullet proof vest and the second wound was a graze on the neck. Police were already looking for two brothers they believe shot the officer. He shielded his eyes with one hand. At least one witness, a nearby building security guard, saw part of the fight and the shooting. Officer Williams had asked for and gotten identification from the two, and at least one ID was found in the vicinity of Williams' patrol car.

Within an hour, police were scouring the town

searching for twenty-five-year-old Henry David Hernandez and his twenty-seven-year-old brother Julian. Still, we were told, it wouldn't be until the brothers were interviewed by police that anyone could be sure how and why the shooting occurred.

Soon I had enough information and videotape to put together a story for the early morning newscast. Against my better judgment, but with no alternative, I got into the news car with Daffy, whose reputation as a wild driver was well-earned, and we sped to the station's downtown studio.

The KMOL-TV station headquarters sits in the heart of San Antonio next to the famous Riverwalk. Owned by United Television, it is the city's oldest television station and still resides in its original building. The story goes that an appliance dealer had bought a bunch of radios, then opened the WOAI radio station to create a market for the new appliance. By 1949, WOAI-TV was started and later the name changed to KMOL after the properties were broken up and sold. WOAI Radio moved its offices and kept the original call letters. KMOL kept the original property and changed its name.

At six A.M. morning anchor Dan Garcia read a short story with videotape, and an interview from police spokesman Paul Buske. My story, which Dan read, said that, "Thirty-seven-year-old Gary Williams is in stable condition at Brook Army Medical Center this morning." Dan also noted the two Hispanic males (whose names had not been "officially" released by the police department) had fought with the officer, stolen his gun and shot him. Police suspected the pair still had the officer's gun.

For the 6:45 A.M. news segment, I lengthened the story and added my voice to the video package. I added new details: the officer had been shot twice, and police said the brothers had removed the officer's gun belt and badge during the fight. The final tag, read by the anchor, informed viewers that one of the brothers was awaiting trial for a 1987 murder charge.

After the morning show, I went into the break room and bought a Coke. Then I walked back to my desk to go over what I knew and what I didn't about the Williams' case. But, a newsroom is unnaturally quiet at 7 A.M. and I wasn't having much luck thinking. So I took my can of caffeine and Daffy's video tape of the crime scene into one of the edit bays and began looking at what he'd shot.

The tape showed the police detectives in their suits searching the area, as well as close up shots of Williams' patrol car, a white cloth of some type, a gun belt, and, of course, the park bench. To be honest, it was a generic video as far as I was concerned. Every shooting I've ever covered had similar shots. There is always a wide-shot of the scene, close up shots of the evidence, police roaming about, and the obligatory interview with a police spokesman.

The only thing that changes are the faces and the individual reaction to the trauma inflicted on the victim. Some of these victims are dead before they get into the ambulance, but even so, the look of death is different on each face.

Williams didn't have that look. The video showed him obviously conscious with a couple of paramedics bending over him inserting I.V.s into his arm.

"He doesn't look bad." The voice was that of José Davilla, our early morning photographer who had walked into the edit booth while I was watching the tape. He stayed as I played back the video tape of Williams in the ambulance for the third time.

"He looks like he's going to be okay," he said.

I shook my head. "I hope so. I've got a call into

the hospital, but so far all they tell me is that he's in surgery and stable."

Davila, like Davenport, has worked at KMOL for years. He's also one of the resident characters on staff. His nickname is D.O.A. and if you ever asked him why he'll likely show you a video tape; you'll end up wishing you'd never seen it.

By 8:30 A.M. Roy Pedroza, the photographer with whom I usually work, and my partner on the crime beat, began making the rounds. Roy, a towering man with a gray beard weighs close to two hundred twenty pounds. His fellow photographers usually call him, "Papa," because of his long association with the station. He can often provide background information that puts stories in their proper perspective.

Our first stop was police headquarters—middle-aged dreary building with the same sort of institutional pallor that affects bureaucracies all across America.

The city spent millions to renovate and redecorate the building. Now many officers joke that with its pale blue and gray tile, the police department looks like a giant urinal. All I can report is some of those arrested have certainly done their best to make it smell like one.

Tucked away in one of the halls used by the city's municipal court in this aging building is the oversized closet the crime beat reporters call the San Antonio Police Department Press Room.

The decor in this office makes it look like Oscar Madison's bedroom. There is a gaping hole in the bottom half of the press room's office door. At one time a screen or steel grate must have been affixed there. Now two pieces of white cardboard that can't seem to stay fully attached to the square hole attempt to provide some privacy.

The Story

Inside the office a single, ancient, black and white television sits on top of a cardboard box adorned with cryptic black humor scrawled by some demented reporter one night. In turn, the television and cardboard box both sit on top of a plain rectangular table on which every manner of newspaper and magazine seems to find its final resting place.

On the wall above the table is a bulletin board which is sometimes home to additional cryptic humor derived from newspaper headlines and photographs, as well as the occasional obligatory dirty joke.

Above the table there are a battery of speakers which constantly inform us as to what's transpiring on the police department's open radio frequencies.

For years, the central feature of this office, other than the half-dozen or so telephones and seemingly thousands of feet of telephone wire, had been a flea infested, yellow couch that was probably picked up off of a curb. It was the site of many a nap when police reporters had nothing else better to do. After *San Antonio Light* reporter Michelle Salcedo took a job with *News Day*, the old worn work-horse of a couch was retired; she graciously saw fit to leave her plush, gray sofa with us. It's a gesture many have never properly thanked her for.

Roy and I stopped at the Press Room to see what the morning gossip on the case was. There was none. The room was empty.

Next, we began walking upstairs to the second floor suite belonging to the public information officers. I expected very little information would be provided to me here. During the nine months I'd worked at KMOL, Paul Buske, who headed the office, and I had gotten into some exhausting battles. He'd stall for days without providing information, or yell openly at me if I'd gone and "got something behind my back," as he put it. Buske, many reporters also feel, is often impossible to live with as a provider of public information.

Many reporters say they can tolerate and even like Buske outside of work. He's a straight arrow, born again, country music loving San Antonio boy who grew up on the city's southside—often thought of as the white, redneck side of town. He has worked in the homicide department and is known as Pablo to his friends.

But he is also known to have many enemies inside the department. He's rumored to be the only sergeant ever forced to drive the police drunk wagon after he angered a Deputy Chief. The night he did, some say the city racked up a record number of drunks arrested in one night.

When Buske became "born again" officers complained he preached too much, although by the time I met him he had given that up. Some officers, though, were convinced the pain of being born twice, when most people only had to do it once, was what put Buske in a bad humor.

Not too long after I met him he was divorced from his wife, and others were convinced going through that was what was making him crabby.

I don't know. But he had a calendar hanging on the wall in his office with the date his divorce would become final circled in red. For the record, I note that he did become a bit easier to talk to after that day passed.

Buske has been involved in most of the battles between local reporters and the police. Many reporters, most especially those at the local newspapers, have complained for years about a lack of cooperation, and arrogance on Buske's part. When they want or need something, especially information that could

The Story

put the police department in a questionable light, Buske will stall and not provide it.

But Buske, who is extremely loyal, "Is in tight," they say, with Police Chief Bill Gibson. The Chief, a level headed and capable administrator values loyalty, perhaps to a fault.

"Are the reports in yet on the shooting?" I asked Buske when I got upstairs to his office.

"What shooting?" he asked me with a grin. (Buske has picked up the reporters' habit of jumping on straight lines.)

"The Gary Williams' shooting." I deadpanned.

"Nothing yet. Lieutenant Ortiz might have something later."

This was Buske's way of telling me that Lieutenant Albert Ortiz, the head of the homicide department, was probably going to have a news conference later.

I asked him to call the station if and when he found out if a news conference would take place. Then I checked to see if anything else had happened overnight that might be newsworthy.

After that, Roy and I left. Our next goal was to talk to the Hernandez family.

Early in the morning police had set up surveillance at the Hernandez residence. Because Williams was the third local policeman shot in as many weeks and because he was shot with his own gun, tension on the police department was palpable. Some of this tension had already spilled over onto the media. Police had threatened a local photographer with jail after he knocked on the Hernandez's front door; so we decided to drive up the road and call the family to see if anyone wanted to talk.

Pulling into Wendy's, a nearby drive-in restaurant, we heard a dispatcher on the police scanner post a bulletin.

"Officer Williams died at 9:47 A.M."

We were both stunned. Williams seemed hurt, but not fatally. He appeared too alert, too sharp to die.

Roy and I proceeded in silence until we got to the pay phone and dialed the telephone number for Henry and Julian's father.

A person with a feminine, youngish voice answered. I figured she was probably related to Henry and Julian.

"Who is this?" she asked.

"My name is Brian Karem. I'm a reporter for Channel Four. I know it's a difficult time right now, but I wonder if I might ask you a few questions?"

"Why don't you tell the police to leave," she cut in.

It was obvious the family, like most San Antonians, recognized the black-walled, tinted windows of the Mercury's and Ford's sitting outside their door as those of San Antonio undercover police officers.

Before I had a chance to answer, she continued, "What the police is saying is all lies," she said excitedly. "The police have the house surrounded. What do they think, that Henry's stupid? That Julian's stupid? Don't you think they'd know the cops are here. They won't come here. Somebody needs to hear their side. They'd tell the truth. But the cops want to kill them that's all . . ." She was now close to hysteria and as I tried to break in I heard the phone wrenched from her.

The sounds of rapid-fire cursing in English and Spanish stung the air. The next voice on the line belonged to a man, older with an agonized, gravelly voice. He turned out to be the father of the fugitives.

"My boys are good boys," he told me. "We had a

party last night and they left. I don't know where they went."

"Could we talk to you on camera sir. I think it's important we get the family's side of this story."

"I don't know," he paused, then went on, "my English isn't so good. I don't know if I want to talk."

"Por favor. Yo creo que lo es necesito." My Spanish wasn't the best; so I motioned for Roy and for the next five minutes we took turns talking to Mr. Hernandez. Finally, he agreed to meet us at Wendy's.

He arrived in a ramshackled car. Slowly he got out. He looked tired, his eyes were red rimmed and blood shot, his salt and pepper beard unshaven.

As we walked to the back of the restaurant's parking lot where Roy set up the camera, he clutched at a brown paper bag which contained a quart of beer.

"My boys are good boys," he told me again.

"I understand. But the police believe they shot a cop last night."

"I know, I know. But they're good boys. Julian, he's been doing so much better. Henry too. They're both good boys. Fathers."

"I understand. But could you tell me what happened last night? Why were they out driving? What were they doing?"

"We had a party yesterday. We had a good time. We drank a lot, but I don't know, I don't know what they were doing . . ." he hung his head and took a swig from the bottle. "They'll never take them."

"I'm sorry, who won't take them?"

"The cops will never take them alive, you know. My boys are good fighters," he paused and stared at me, "if they have to be." He shook his head, "Nobody's gonna hear their side of this—"

I broke in, "Well, you know, that's what the girl on the phone said a few minutes ago."

"What girl?" Henry and Julian's father quickly looked up from his bottle, having taken another swig.

"The girl that answered the telephone at your house a few minutes ago."

"Don't talk to her," his voice tightened, "she's got nothing to do with this. You want something, you talk to me."

"Sure." I didn't understand the sudden anger. It could've been a sudden surge of male dominance, or something different. I decided to skip over it. "Do you think if your boys are arrested, they'd let us talk to them?"

"I don't know. But if they are, I'll let them know you'll talk to them."

Handing him a business card, I thanked him. In the five minutes we'd been talking he'd already finished his beer. Now he was fumbling with the strap on his white overalls. Even though it was still morning, he was obviously hungover or drunk and having a hard time with the news that his boys were wanted for killing a cop.

As we left, Roy and I talked about what we had. It wasn't much. I did know that the brothers had been partying, Julian and Henry had a family, and the father didn't want me talking to anyone but him. He claimed he didn't know why his sons were out driving; so I was not much further along in my pursuit of the story at 11 A.M. than I had been shortly after sunrise.

A short time later, I tracked down a detective friend, who with the help of his computer terminal, was able to provide me with a composite biographical sketch of Henry and Julian. Buske said the department wouldn't officially talk about the pair's past, but I, like most other police reporters, knew someone who *would* provide that information.

It showed that Henry had been arrested several

times. His last arrest was for murder, and, prior to that, he had been arrested for aggravated assault with a deadly weapon. His brother Julian had also been arrested several times. However, his latest arrest stemmed from a driving-while-intoxicated charge—his first DWI offense.

By lunch hour, Tom Edwards, a police reporter for *The Express News*, was guessing that the police were not telling us everything about the shooting. Most everyone in the press corps agreed with that. After all, we really only knew that the police officer had been shot after a violent struggle, and that detectives wanted the Hernandez brothers for the shooting. There had been some ugly talk among some of the officers on the street that they would extract street justice for the shooting. "An eye for an eye," one of them had said. But nothing else had been heard, so far.

Edwards suggested that Henry probably did the shooting. "He's got the violent criminal past, not his brother," he told me. "I'd lay odds on it."

I shrugged my shoulders. It wasn't that I didn't trust Tom, I did; I just didn't have enough information to comment. I cast a lingering glance his way. Maybe Tom did. After all he got the first major scoop on the Williams' shooting. Pulling some strings, he managed to procure a photograph of the slain officer and *The San Antonio Express News*, consequently, was the only paper to print it. That may sound like a small victory, but in San Antonio it is a major scoop. Although other states allow the police to release photographs of officers, the state of Texas does not. San Antonio police have always been notoriously strict in following a state law the San Antonio Police Union helped to write.

Tom also found out that getting the story in San Antonio can sometimes *make* you the story. After getting the photograph, the rival newspaper in town, the

San Antonio Light, ran an article questioning Tom's ethics because he'd been able to get Williams' photograph. I turned my attention back to the business at hand.

This shooting was puzzling. I still hadn't found out much about it. I decided to follow up on Tom's evaluation of who had actually pulled the trigger, and contact the brothers' attorney Joe Hernandez (no relation).

It wasn't until late in the afternoon that Roy and I were able to track him down. Joe turned out to be as evasive as the two fugitive brothers, but he did confirm some things in the pair's background.

"You know there's been some talk that the police might shoot these two guys if they find them," I reminded him.

"I'd heard that," he told me quietly.

"Have you talked to them since the shooting, Joe?"

"You know I can't talk to you about that."

"Yes. But, if you had, do you think anyone will ever find out their side of the story?"

"I think I can say that it might be pretty interesting, knowing these two the way I do."

That was hard to figure. I didn't know if what Joe told me was pure conjecture, or if he had actually talked to the brothers and I'm sure he wanted it that way.

By late afternoon, I was visibly tired. I'd been on the story since before dawn, hadn't had any lunch, and still had to put together a story for the 5 P.M. newscast. I had already handed off a reaction piece story to Cheryl Emerson, a solid reporter with more than ten years of experience. After the 5 P.M. show I was going to hand off everything to nightside reporter, and one of the station's weekend anchors: Susan Tejeda.

The Story

As I struggled to meet my afternoon deadline, I got a call from a friend of mine at the police department.

"You working on the Hernandez story?" he asked.

"Of course. That's the story of the day."

"What a shame you're dropping the ball."

I thought about that comment for a second. Was I being teased? Who knew? By this time of the afternoon my mind was mush and my police friend knew it. I decided he was kidding. I had worked hard all day long and figured I had as much information as anyone else on the Hernandez brothers. But I bit.

"What do you mean dropping the ball?"

He chuckled and went on. "I just think it's a shame that the Hernandez brothers are going to turn themselves in at the front desk and KMOL won't be there."

This is not the kind of information a reporter likes to hear less than two hours from news time with his story already in the can. It has the same effect as snapping on a dog's choke collar. Of course, I asked the first thing that popped into my head.

"Any other television stations know about this?"

"Not yet," he murmured, further whetting my appetite.

It didn't take me long to hang up the telephone and grab Roy who drove like a madman to the police department.

We got there, and, of course, everyone on the police beat had already heard the rumor. We were the last to arrive. Obviously, the Hernandez brothers didn't know there was a party planned for them. They never showed.

At 5 P.M. Monday, March 27th, KMOL aired what was basically the police version of the shooting.

Cheryl Emerson put together a side bar story which contained reaction (some would later say knee-jerk reaction) from Mayor Henry Cisneros. He wondered if the police needed more training and perhaps were being too judicious in their use of deadly force. Finally, the station included a part of the interview with Julian Hernandez Sr. He said he last saw his boys at an Easter party the previous night. He told the camera that after he heard about the shooting he'd been up crying all night.

After the newscast, I had strongly ambivalent feelings. I'd gotten all the essential facts and—looking at the other stations—knew I hadn't been beat on the story. But still, when it was all added up, the coverage was remarkably one-sided. No one had even interviewed the only witness police said existed: the security guard. The story was heavily weighted in favor of the police department's version, and while there was no reason to doubt it, I and other reporters found ourselves still searching for independent confirmation of the facts.

I shrugged my shoulders and recapped most everything for Susan Tejeda, who would be doing the ten o'clock news. A young, pretty woman with dark hair and dark eyes, Tejeda could be tenacious when covering a story.

On the newscast Tejeda fleshed out the prior history of the Hernandez brothers and took the "revolving door" of justice approach to the story. She outlined how Julian had spent some time at the Texas Department of Corrections, and how his younger brother Henry was charged with the shooting death of a thirty-three year old man in September of 1987. She went on to say how Henry was awaiting trial for that as well as an attempted murder charge, but was released on a fifteen thousand dollar bond. Tejeda talked to Fred Rodriguez the district attorney, and Lieutenant Albert Ortiz (who finally decided to talk to the press), then she went back to Joe Hernandez and talked to him again. Her story concluded that everyone close to the pair hoped they would surrender.

By that time the newspaper reporters were again assembled at the police station. Another rumor had surfaced and again many of us thought that the Hernandez brothers would turn themselves in. Daffy covered for KMOL while I, exhausted by now, went home to sleep for a few hours. It made no difference, because the Hernandez brothers once more did not show up.

Chapter 3

''Gang Bang''

At 5:30 the next morning, I got into the office and began scanning the newspapers to see if I'd missed much. I hadn't. Both local papers had printed more than the television and radio stations had aired; but, we all had essentially the same story.

Shortly after 8 A.M., Roy and I began our rounds again. Usually our routine requires us to stop in at most of the major law enforcement offices and talk with secretaries, managers, and just about anyone else of interest we see. Sometimes we go out to lunch with our contacts, sometimes we just talk and not necessarily about "a story."

On March 28th, 1989, however, we did not have the luxury of idle conversation and knew there would be little. Our first stop of the day was again Paul Buske.

Buske, on this morning, was at his non-cooperative best. More than a day after the shooting the police weren't officially saying any more than they had the day before.

Buske expressed concern over the safety of the police in the street and said the Hernandez brothers should turn themselves in. Another police officer said the Hernandez brothers would probably be shot while the police "attempted to arrest the subjects." A third officer told me the possible shooting of the Hernandez brothers was "advanced concepts in law enforcement," a term I'd usually heard in San Antonio when cops were talking about one crook killing another.

Roy kept Buske busy while I tried to find others in the department who could provide additional information about Williams and the shooting. We've often employed this tactic to keep Buske unaware of what we were doing.

In the previous months before this shooting, Buske refused to supply information to reporters that courts and state law said we could have. This prompted seemingly never ending appeals to the State Attorney General to end the charade, but nothing ever seemed to be done about it.

I filled out a request for the audio tapes of the Gary Williams' case in Burke's office:

Dear Chief Gibson:

I would respectfully request access to open records: that is, the tape transmission of Officer Gary Williams' conversation with his dispatcher prior to and during the events that led to his loss of life.

As this information is already an open record and the media has access to this frequency, I would ask for immediate access to the records as the police department is the official custodian of these records.

Brian J. Karem
For KMOL-TV

Buske logged it in March 27th, 1989 at 11:48 A.M. Marcy Walker, KSAT-TV's longtime police reporter, filed her request about the same time I did. Both of us became furious when Buske told us once again the department planned to request an Attorney General's opinion.

Buske—even when confronted by a united and angry press and Superior Court decision—refused to cooperate.

"I don't need you," he told me. "You all are still number three in the ratings."

A short while after Buske made his disparaging remark, Dr. Susan Dana, the good natured, petite woman who is Chief Assistant to Dr. Vincent Dimaio, the Bexar County Medical Examiner began Gary Williams' autopsy.

Dr. Dana conducts most of the county autopsies. Some believe her to be a bit strange because she claims to thoroughly love her work.

As many as four bodies at a time can be cut open and examined in the autopsy room. With a bone saw she must cut open the skull and remove the brain. With huge shears, the chest cavity is carved open in a Y-shape. The organs are removed and weighed. Blood is drawn. Wounds are examined. Bullets are removed.

All of this is done with meticulous care, not only so the cause of death can be determined, but also to protect the doctor from accidentally being infected with the AIDS virus.

After tissue and blood samples are taken, and only after Dr. Dana is satisfied she has thoroughly examined the deceased, all the organs are unceremoniously dumped back into the open chest cavity.

Sometimes a technician must force the innards back into the cavity and sew the wound shut with what appears to be a rope. Afterward the corpse is hosed off and wheeled back into a large cooler where it is kept company by the remains of others who've died during the last twenty-four hours.

"All people are equal in death," Dr. Dana says.

And so it was with Gary Williams. His body was kept in the cooler until 1:30 P.M. on March 27th, 1989.

The body had all the classic marks on it from emergency trauma surgery, including needle marks, surgical cuts, and plastic tubes.

Other than that, she noted how bruised and battered Gary was from his fight with Henry. He had cuts and bruises on his knees, elbows, arms, legs, and he also had a black eye. But the two most notable wounds were a bullet hole in his left chest almost parallel with his navel and a quarter of an inch of missing skin on his neck that Dr. Dana concluded was an extremely nasty bite wound.

Upon closer examination of the bullet wound, Dr. Dana found out just how unlucky Gary Williams had been. To begin with the bullet struck at an extremely oblique angle which had enabled it to go under the officer's bullet proof vest. Dr. Dana knew this from the skin that had been furrowed up by the bullet as it plowed into Gary's abdomen. Because the bullet had entered at such an extreme angle it ripped up through his colon, pancreas, small bowel, stomach, spleen, left lung and came to rest in his spinal column.

"The poor bastard," another doctor would later comment. "If he'd been shot straight on, he might have lived even if he hadn't been wearing a bulletproof vest. The bullet probably would have gone straight through him. But the way he was shot, the bullet ripped through most of his vital organs and he bled to death. He never really had a chance."

Dr. Dana noted everything and per well established protocol, she took a sample of what little blood was left in the body. The blood tests might take weeks to complete, but by late in the afternoon on the 27th, most of the hard work was done. For an autopsy of a policeman felled by a fatal gunshot wound, nothing seemed out of the ordinary. There was no reason to suspect the blood tests would show anything surprising.

By mid-afternoon Roy and I had still gotten nowhere. For a while we staked out the attorney's office, hoping maybe the Hernandez brothers would show up. We hung around several hours but there was no noticeable traffic. So we headed back to the station. Ironically almost as soon as we left the Hernandez brothers arrived and turned themselves in to their attorney.

Shortly before the 5 o'clock news, Joe Vasquez, the assignment editor, fielded a telephone call. For the umpteenth time, rumors had been floating around that the brothers would turn themselves in. Now, the district attorney was confirming it. He was planning to take custody of Henry and Julian Hernandez. The media was invited to watch and take pictures. I made it over to the district attorney's office in no time.

Tension was high; about a dozen armed security guards in suits hustled the Hernandez brothers down the hall to be magistrated before presiding Judge James Barlow.

It was a typical "Gang Bang"—the term reporters use to describe mass confusion with cameras present.

Joe Hernandez, the brothers' attorney, was afraid some police officer might take a pot-shot at Julian and Henry before they could go to trial. So, before he would agree to allow the district attorney's men to come to his office and accept Henry and Julian's surrender he had insisted on security—lots of it. Fred Rodriguez had reluctantly agreed.

The pair had been taken into custody, the media notified, and then came the walk across the courthouse hallway from the D.A.'s office to the judge's chambers.

Henry and Julian looked like they'd worn the same clothes for the last two days. Both had long, unkempt hair. They strode quietly and defiantly across the hall, yet a glimmer of fear passed across each of their faces as they confronted the great spectacle of reporters, cops, and lawyers assembled to witness their surrender.

They dodged questions and kept their heads up. Once, Henry darted a glance back at the glass doors of the district attorney's office to see members of his family assembled there.

Inside the courtroom Joe Hernandez told presiding Judge James Barlow that his clients, ". . . request they not be interviewed by any members of the police department and without counsel being present. We ask the court to enforce that, particularly."

Again, I had an uneasy feeling. Although the pair had turned themselves in, it was clear that the District Attorney hadn't interrogated them. No one had heard their side of the story except their own attorney.

After being magistrated, the same armed guards quietly began to escort the Hernandez brothers back to the D.A.'s office.

Suddenly, the scene turned to bedlam. One of the security guards pushed me into a nearby chair and ripped my suit and a KENS T.V. photographer was pushed into a wall, while a female reporter nearly had her arm ripped from its socket by the D.A.'s men. They made it clear that while the media were invited to this party, we weren't going to be tolerated.

Interviewed after the Hernandez brothers left,

Joe Hernandez and District Attorney Fred Rodriguez said the added security had been necessary because of a concern for Henry and Julian's safety.

"I find it a little ironic that Joe Hernandez was asking me for help," Rodriguez told the assembled reporters. "He didn't want them harmed. I told him, 'Joe, I'm going to do a little more than harm them. I'm probably going to kill them. I'm going to ask for the death penalty.'"

Members of the Hernandez family stood by and watched with agonized faces from a quiet alcove in the district attorney's office. Through the glass doors they stared at Julian and Henry being paraded through the halls, saw the reporters shouting endless questions and they wondered too, when Julian and Henry would be free again.

But, above all, the family wanted Julian and Henry to get their story out.

"I told them to surrender," their mother, Rosie, said. "I thought it would be better so they could prove their innocence. Everything in the paper was wrong. The police made mistakes too."

She looked haggard and appeared to have been crying. Her two boys were gone and she had no idea when or if they would be coming back.

By six that night I was back at the station determined to learn what really happened at the Burger Boy the day before. The best way to find out, I thought, was to get an interview with both Hernandez brothers and see what they would say. But, that now looked to be a remote possibility since they were in jail.

Still, I decided to give it a try. I called Alex Ramirez, the chief deputy for the Bexar County Sheriff's Department and a fairly good news source.

"I don't think it can be done," Alex said.

"Don't make any final decisions yet," I pleaded. "I'm on my way over."

"Don't bother, I'm sure the Sheriff will say no," he told me.

"Well, maybe I can persuade you both with my diplomatic charm and suave personality."

We both laughed.

Minutes later I was at the Bexar County Jail. I walked through the big, glass doors and saw Alex standing just outside of his office talking to the Sheriff.

"So Alex, can I talk to them or what?" I tried to be affable.

"I don't think so. I talked with the Sheriff and he says no."

Alex knew the Sheriff better than I did and would probably have better luck with him—that is, if I could convince Alex to let me interview the Hernandez brothers.

I followed Alex into his office and tried again.

"Alex, I'd like to get these guys on camera. Can't you just bring them downstairs for five minutes?"

"No," he said sharply. "That's against policy!"

I pressed him, "Alex, I've heard these guys want to talk to a reporter. Is there any way I can just *talk* to them on the telephone? Can't I *call* them?"

There was a hint of amusement in his eyes. "No, but there are telephones in the cell. They can call you."

I gave him my most engaging smile. "They don't know me. How can I let them know I want to talk to them? Can't I just get my business card to them?" I pulled out a card. "Come on, Alex. I really need this one."

Alex looked at my card, then back at me.

"Look, if they want to call you, we can't stop it. I'll check with the boss."

Harlon Copeland, Bexar County Sheriff, is about as close to the clichéd Texas Sheriff as one can get in a living, breathing sentient human being. He's a tall man, in his fifties with graying hair. He prefers two types of music; country and western.

In the three years I've known him, I've never seen Harlon without a pair of pointed-toed cowboy boots complete with matching cowboy hat. He has the large belly that seems to be needed by most county sheriffs in Texas, and right at the highest point on his belly sits a gold and silver belt buckle. It looks like if you pulled off the buckle Harlon might jet across the room like a balloon whose air was suddenly let out.

There have been dozens of stories told about Harlon, and because of his personality many have taken on the air of legend, but many of these are true; including the time he accused a Texas governor of snorting coke.

Once Harlon had a riot in his jail. But, he didn't want to call it that; it might encourage the inmates, he said.

"It was a butt-kicking contest and we won," Harlon explained instead.

On another occasion Harlon thought he saw one of his patrol officers driving with a patrol car's emergency flashers on when there was no need for that officer to be driving in such a manner. The sheriff knew people would never stand for this; so since he couldn't identify the officer, he just called all the officers in from that part of the county and fired every one of them.

He had a change of heart when he realized that would leave a lot of the county without any police protection.

The list goes on, but suffice it to say, Harlon is a character. And, as Alex went next door to the sheriff's office, I had no idea what Harlon's response would be to my inquiry.

There's a running joke inside Harlon's administrative offices that they live by "the rules of the day." In other words, what Harlon says is law on Monday is not necessarily what Harlon says is law on Tuesday.

So I was surprised and relieved when Alex came back and handed me a yellow post-it note pad.

"Here," he said. "Just write your name and the number you want them to call you at on the pad. Your card's too confusing."

I laughed, wrote down my name and number on the note pad and handed it back to him.

"Look, I'll give them this note, but I'm going to tell them it's up to them whether they want to talk to you. I'm not going to make them."

I nodded, "That's fine, Alex. I'm sure they want to talk."

I wasn't exactly sure, but I did have hope.

Alex walked out of his office, presumably for the bowels of the jail. He returned about ten minutes later and told me to go back to the office and wait for a 7:10 P.M. telephone call.

"The thing is, the one brother doesn't want to talk," Alex said.

"Which one wants to?"

"I think it's Henry that wants to talk. But Julian doesn't want to. He told his brother to do the talking."

"Thanks, Alex," I said as I turned to leave.

"Hey, Brian. I did tell them not to talk to you."

I stopped and turned back to him. "Okay. But he wants to talk, right?"

"Yeah. And I told him it was up to him if he wanted to. I don't want anyone thinking I'm making this guy talk to you."

"Fine, I'm a big boy. I'll handle that. As long as he calls I think I can get him to talk to me."

I glanced down at my watch. It was time to leave. I had about fifteen minutes before the telephone call, according to Alex, and I still had to drive back to the station and set up a recorder so we could use the Hernandez interview on television.

"Hold it." Alex gently grabbed me by the arm. "One more thing. I don't want my name attached to any of this. All right?"

"You don't know anything about this case, do you, Alex?"

"No."

"Well, what's the problem? I mean, why don't you want your name attached to it?"

"I'd just rather not have this office go through any more than we have to, if you know what I mean."

I nodded. I knew exactly what he meant. Copeland, with his aggressive personality and by virtue of the fact that he was a high ranking republican public official in a city filled with nothing but democrats, often got into political scrapes.

I also knew that Alex seemed concerned. He'd done me a favor, now, Alex was asking me for a personal favor in return. He wanted me to respect his confidentiality. I did.

However, I also agreed to keep Alex out of it, because I believed if I got Hernandez on tape it wouldn't much matter how I got in touch with him. Realistically Henry could always reveal who the person was; so it didn't seem like a big deal to offer Alex confidentiality. That was to be my first mistake, but by no means my last.

I returned to the station and we all celebrated my potential interview until we realized we really had no way to capture a telephone conversation in the newsroom. Then the news room flew into a flurry of action. Bob Sullivan, the operation's manager, and a man who had gained the reputation of having an answer to everything promised, "I'll come up with something."

In the next half hour much duct tape and wire were produced. Someone came up with an audio-cassette tape recorder and someone else found an audio-cassette tape. Just before seven, finally, everything was in place. We all waited anxiously for the 7:10 deadline.

But at 7:15, there was still no phone call.

Nervous, I called Alex Ramirez. The call was coming, he assured me. A guard would place it.

While we scrambled at KMOL to set things up, Henry Hernandez was having his own problems. Accused of Capitol Murder, he had begun the day a free, but hunted man. Now he was in the Bexar County Jail where he had been remanded without bond.

During the afternoon he had been dragged from one end of the county courthouse to the other. Twice he had faced the local press. They had peppered him with questions, shouting at him and Julian. He'd done as Joe Hernandez had requested and hadn't talked to any of them. But their attitude riled him. They made him out to be a cold-blooded murderer and worse, they'd accused his brother of things he hadn't done.

That was eating at him as well. None of this would've happened if he and Julian hadn't been fighting, and Henry couldn't help but feel guilty for getting his brother mixed up in this mess. But Henry didn't know where to turn next. He was confused and upset. To make matters worse, the guards had separated him from Julian and Henry was now unable to talk with his older brother.

Then, as he sat in the holding cell waiting for his permanent housing assignment in the jail's maximum security wing, he noticed a well groomed dark haired man in a dark blue suit, with an air of authority about him.

He heard the man asking where the Hernandez brothers were, and watched several guards nodding deprecatingly to him as they pointed out Julian's and Henry's separate holding cells. The man strolled over to Julian and talked with him for a few minutes. Then he made his way to Henry's cell.

Henry, even in his confused state of mind, knew the man had to be important, but he had no idea he was about to meet the jail's chief deputy.

Introducing himself Alex gave Henry the yellow, post-it note pad.

"Your brother Julian doesn't want to talk to the media, but if you want to, then you can call," he said.

Henry hesitated for a minute or two wondering whether he should talk to a reporter. Still he wanted to tell them they were getting the story all wrong.

He picked up the telephone with sweating hands. First he called his parents' house. He talked with his cousin, Debra Ledesma, and explained how confused he felt. Then he had her place the call to KMOL while he stayed on the line.

Moments later, even as I was talking to Alex on the telephone and wondering if I would ever get to speak with Henry, he and his cousin got through to our station.

"Stay on the phone," Henry begged Debra.

She did.

"Brian, I got a call for you." Joe shouted in the news room.

Hanging up with Alex I told Joe, "Transfer it into the edit-bay."

When the phone rang there, I picked it up.

"Hello."

"Is this the reporter?" a husky voiced person who identified himself as a prison guard asked.
"Yes."
"Hold on for Henry Hernandez."

Chapter 4

The Interview

"Hello," Henry Hernandez softly stuttered in his thick Hispanic accent. I could barely hear him and was afraid our attempts to record a conversation with him would be a dismal failure. I had little faith in the small, taped up, black plastic box with all the wires protruding from it that was supposed to record our lead story for the night. I motioned to Bob Sullivan that I couldn't hear Henry. From two edit booths away, he motioned back that he understood and would correct the problem. Then I returned to Henry.

"I'm back, Henry. Can you speak up a little bit? I can barely hear you."

"Okay. The thing is, sir," he stuttered again, fiercely this time, "my, my attorney has advised me not to say nothing. And the, the detectives tell me not to say nothing. But, I've gotta say something, because every, everything that was in the news was wrong. Every, every;" he took a deep breath and began again, "the only thing that everybody did was only take one person's story. You know?"

I certainly agreed with him on that score. I didn't know a police reporter in town who wasn't struggling to make sense out of what little we'd been told.

I looked out of the edit booth and saw Bob give me the "thumbs up" signal. I assumed that meant he was recording the audio with no problem. I turned my attention back to Henry.

". . . You know, things didn't happen that way, sir. Ah, ah, this officer, he was in some kind of a rowdy mood or something like that, and you know, he just, he went out of control. You know. And I was just defending myself."

Joe, who had been standing behind me in the edit booth, listening to the conversation, broke in.

"Yeah. Sure. How can he claim police brutality? The cop got shot with his own gun."

I shook my head. I wasn't impressed with Henry's claim, in fact, I figured it was the same speech everyone makes when arrested. But, once again discordant thoughts flashed through my mind about the fight he'd had with Gary Williams. How could Williams lose his gun to a skinny little kid who was several inches shorter and about thirty pounds lighter than he was? Of course, the obvious answer was that Julian had been helping his brother. But as we talked, Henry said Julian had been knocked out of things early with a well placed blow to the head from Williams' service revolver, the one that moments later took the officer's life.

I knew Henry could be lying to protect his brother; willing to take the fall to let Julian go free. But, if Henry was telling the truth, I thought, then something really didn't add up here.

"Who pulled the trigger?" I asked him.

"Excuse me." Again the politeness. Several times Henry had called me "sir." He obviously didn't deal with reporters very much. We get called a lot of things, but "sir" generally isn't one of them.

"Who pulled the trigger?" I asked again.

"I did. But, because, because he, he was gonna . . ." his voice trailed off so soft again, his words were barely audible. I heard the sharp intake of his breath, and then his voice was new, stronger, "You know shoot me."

There was a telling moment of silence. Then, Henry went on, the officer had pulled the gun on him, had threatened to shoot him, and then the two had started to struggle. Henry clawed at and bit Williams.

Finally, Henry said, the officer had tried to shoot him. Henry grabbed the gun and a shot went over his shoulder. As the two struggled for the gun, Henry got hold of it. The fatal shot went off as the two fought and fell to the ground. Then Henry mumbled, "The officer said something like, 'You can go home now.'"

The remark seemed meaningless. "Are you sorry this happened?" I concluded.

"Yes, I'm very sorry it happened, 'cause I didn't wanna do it. But this officer gave me no choice."

I hung up the telephone. Although Debra Ledesma had been on the line, I never knew it.

I turned to Joe. He gave me a "high-five," and I controlled the sudden desire to dance on desk tops. Bob came out of his make-shift audio booth grinning like a large, flaccidly happy cheshire cat. He held up the recorder.

"Got it," was all he said.

We, indeed, had a story. Henry Hernandez had confessed to pulling the trigger and claimed he did it in self-defense. He contradicted the official police version of the story by saying he'd only shot the officer once, and by saying his brother Julian had nothing to do with the fight or the fatal shooting.

"You believe what he said?" Joe asked.

"I don't know." I shook my head, "He was a little confused about how his brother was involved and I'm not sure he isn't fudging some of this to get his brother off the hook. But when he talks about the fight and the shooting, it's almost like he's reliving it. I don't think he made that stuff up."

I walked over to my desk and began putting the story together. First, I gave a list of the quotes I planned to use in the piece to Bob. He had to take the audio recording up to the production studio to take some of the white noise out of the tape, so we could use the interview in our newscast. Then, I called a friend of mine over at the *Express News* and arranged to get a copy of the photograph of Gary Williams since the police department was still refusing to release a copy to the press.

Finally, I was ready to begin writing. Then the telephone rang in the newsroom and once again Joe yelled across the newsroom for me.

"Brian, it's Henry."

"Henry who?" My mind was on putting together the story; I wasn't making the connection.

"Henry the plumber, who do you think? Henry Hernandez!"

I wasn't the only one to jump. Jorge Saenz, the photographer who had helped Bob Sullivan record the first conversation, began scrambling around to find the tape recorder. Then Joe paged Bob to get him back from production and I picked up the telephone.

"Henry?"

"Yeah, I want to talk to you some more about this officer."

I watched as Jorge, Bob, and Joe struggled to get the recorder set up again. At the same time I tried to listen to Henry.

"What, what about the officer, Henry?"

"Well, he was in some kind of rowdy mood. He

beat me and my brother with his flashlight or blackjack or something. My brother was in the car."

"The whole time?"

"What? No. Not the whole time. But this officer, he was like drugged . . ."

Suddenly I heard a different voice on the telephone. A young woman, whose voice sounded vaguely familiar, began a barrage of questions.

"Have you investigated the cop for police brutality? Did he have a background on that? Is there anyway you could find out?"

"Who is this? Who's on the other line?" I said.

It was Debra, Henry's cousin who had facilitated his first call to me. She reintroduced herself. I wrote down her name in my reporter's notebook and asked her for a telephone number so I could call her back and find out more about the Hernandezs' past.

"Are you going to help us?" she asked agitatedly.

"Listen, Laura," I said, glancing down at the wrong name I'd written in my note pad. "I'm going to look at everything. I promise you that."

By this time Bob and Jorge had the tape recorder functioning; so I asked her if she minded being recorded.

"Are we being recorded?"

"Yes. We've recorded most of this. Do you want to be recorded?"

Henry spoke up, "Go right ahead."

While we talked some more, Dino Chiecchi from the *Express News* walked in holding up Gary Williams' picture.

"Who are you on the phone with?" he asked.

I couldn't hold back a grin, "Henry Hernandez."

"No shit, man!"

"No. I'm talking to him right now."

The Interview

"Ask him where the gun is, man."

I turned to listen as Henry continued to talk about Gary Williams' brutal attitude in front of the Burger Boy.

"You're saying the cop had a bad attitude?" I asked Henry.

Without hesitation and in the same quiet voice, Henry insisted, "Yes. The, ah, the officer had a real bad attitude. Yeah. It wasn't like prejudice or anything, it was like as if he was angry—you know—he just wanted to punch somebody and hit them and hit them."

I decided to work in Dino's question. The police had been searching for the gun and hadn't yet found it.

"Henry, let me ask you: where's the gun now?"

"I don't know."

"Who had it?"

"I had it."

"What did you do with it?"

"I threw it."

Dino stayed until I was through. When I hung up the telephone just a couple of minutes later, he turned to me.

"That's a hell of a story, man," Dino said. "I'm going over to the house to talk to the family. I'll let you know what they say." He left, saying he was going to follow up.

By 8:30 P.M. it became clear, through the efforts of Bob, Jorge, and myself that we had a major story. It was also equally obvious that nothing like this had ever been tried at KMOL before. There was no precedent for this type of story and no pattern to follow in keeping notes or audio tape or anything pertaining to the story. I knew it would cause a stir, but had no idea how big.

I did know, though, how the station would play the story. Off the top of the 10 P.M. newscast anchor Alan Hemberger announced that police still weren't sure who had shot thirty-seven year old police officer Gary Williams. "But in this exclusive report, twenty-five year old Henry David Hernandez tells our Brian Karem he pulled the trigger in self-defense."

Then, for about two minutes we broadcast excerpts from Henry's interview in a taped package that I narrated.

At KMOL, we were convinced the story advanced the public's knowledge of the shooting in ways the police department had been unable to. Henry had contradicted police reports, saying that the first shot fired went over Henry's head in the struggle for the gun; it hadn't grazed the officer's neck. Henry also said that the officer had "some kind of attitude," and that something was wrong with him. Finally, Henry insisted his brother was innocent of any wrongdoing. According to Henry, Julian had been in the police car when the shooting occurred.

After the newscast I went over my notes. In the rush to get everything done, I hadn't taken down anything of a comprehensive nature. All I had written down were the names of Ramirez, the Sheriff, and Laura (alias Debra). I also had Debra's telephone number on the pad, so I added the Sheriff's and Alex's numbers to it, in case I needed to contact them.

I doodled carelessly on my note pad and started to think about where I would take the story on Wednesday. It was apparent that I still had to flesh out Henry's and Julian's past. Debra had promised to do that, and told me I could call her that night.

Of course, I needed to check on Gary Williams again. But, I had made a call earlier in the morning to the Police Civil Service Commission. The commission keeps track of all disciplinary acts against police officers and makes those decisions known to the public. There was nothing outstanding in Williams' file, but perhaps, I'd missed something.

I had about ten minutes to contemplate all this before I got a call from Dino Chiecchi who had shown up at the Hernandez home when the newscast had aired.

"The family says that isn't Henry," he told me.

"What?" I almost dropped the telephone.

"The sister says Henry doesn't stutter like that and the rest of the family isn't sure that it's Henry you talked to.

I choked back a very real case of panic. Had I taken all the precautions necessary to ensure I'd actually talked with Henry Hernandez? I trusted Alex Ramirez and knew he wouldn't intentionally fool me, but had I been too anxious to get the interview? If I was wrong and had spoken to someone other than Henry it was the worst and probably last mistake of my career. I thought about our celebration at KMOL: the grins, the urges to dance on desk tops and the high fives I'd done in the newsroom. What a fool I was.

Finally, I got hold of myself and told Chiecchi that I was sure I had talked with Hernandez. I remembered Alex Ramirez getting on the telephone, the guard getting on the telephone, and then finally Hernandez. Still, had something gone wrong? I hurried home, arriving shortly after 11 P.M. in a state of confusion, scared for my professional life.

Fumbling through my notebook, I found Debra's number and called her. She made no attempt to assure me I had been talking to Henry Hernandez.

"He stutters differently. He didn't stutter on the telephone like he does at home," she said.

"Was it him or not?"

"Are you going to look and see if that cop was involved in police brutality?" she asked again.

"It will be part of whatever story I work on," I promised. "But," I said, "will you sign an affidavit with my attorney, which states that to the best of your knowledge I had talked to Henry Hernandez on the telephone that night?"

She wouldn't sign a statement; however, she calmed my fears somewhat by constantly referring to the guy to whom I had spoken on the telephone as Henry.

Finally, her reasons became clear.

"I didn't like what you did on television," she said.

Now, I understood the root of her discontent.

"I'm sorry," I said. "I thought we were quite fair."

"You cut everything up. You didn't include everything he said."

"Laura," I said, still using the name on my note pad, "I couldn't do that. We only had two minutes on the air and the conversation lasted a lot longer. I just tried to use the best stuff."

Without correcting me on the use of her name, she conceded that she understood that. Then, she asked me if I needed to know anything else.

For the next twenty minutes we talked about Henry, Julian, and their previous charges. She told me what she knew about their life; who their friends were, what establishments they frequented, and who I should talk to about them.

Afterwards, she told me she didn't get along too well with the family because of her husband.

"Henry's father gets real mad at me sometimes," she offered.

"Listen, I don't think anyone is going to know you talked to me unless Henry tells them."

"Well, please, I just don't want to cause any more trouble for the family. They might take it out on my husband."

"Do you not want me to mention that I talked with you?"

I asked slowly. I was having a hard time understanding her concern. Henry had called her and she had called me for him. She had given me some information, in the last few minutes, which might lead to something but not that much. Her fears seemed irrational.

"Just don't tell anyone we talked with each other."

That seemed an easy enough request. Henry was the source for the statements he'd made. Debra was no more than a conduit as Alex had been.

I considered the promise of confidentiality for a few moments more and asked a few more questions. Again she told me she had trouble with the family because of her husband. He was an Iranian or Libyan and the family wasn't too fond of him. Apparently she was worried about backlash against her because of him. If I extended to her an agreement of confidentiality it wouldn't harm anyone in any way and would put her mind at ease. She did, after all, provide me with some background information on Henry and Julian that would lead to other stories. She also told me some things about each of the men that the family probably wouldn't want the public to know.

I weighed the risks and decided once again that the majority of the real information had been given to me by Henry, not his cousin nor the people at the Sheriff's department.

It seemed logical and proper to protect all of

them because perhaps they could provide me with more information in the future. I've probably done the same thing with different sources hundreds of times and nothing has ever come of it.

So after, I promised Debra I wouldn't tell anybody about her involvement in the story. I didn't lose much sleep thinking about it.

Of course, not much that night could cause me to lose sleep. It had been a long two days.

Chapter 5

Alamo Heat

San Antonio, Texas, in the vernacular of a reporter, is a "good" news town. That is to say, that seldom a day goes by without a police chase, shooting, drug deal, or something extremely visual and nasty to cover. The city eats such scenes up, or at least the viewing public does.

There's a certain paradox to this, since the city prides itself on being a tourist mecca. Yet, scratch the surface of this town, and you'll see the blood that flowed from the Alamo still taints daily life in what is now known as the Alamo City. It is a curious town which thrives on violence. No one is immune to it and no one escapes from it.

The police have battled the violently, macho spirit for years, even though in many ways the department is part of it.

Nothing brought that home a few years ago more than the Tucker-Smith case. That one case, involving police officers Ferrell Tucker and Steven Smith, would forever change how the city looked at its officers. It dramatically changed the way the police department does business and the shock waves from that case are felt to this very day.

Stephen Smith, an upper middle-class San Antonio progeny from Alamo Heights (home to the city's yuppie enclave), became a member of the San Antonio Police Department in 1979.

His best friend and co-worker, Ferrell Tucker, gunned him down in Smith's own Chevy Chevette in 1986. Between the years of 1979 to 1986 Smith became a vigilante killer, hunting down people he thought deserved to be shot, then acting as judge, jury and self-appointed executioner.

Officially, Smith was responsible for only three killings, but privately the police concede there may have been more. In fact some police officers have grimly joked that Smith was personally responsible for the old murder rate record in 1982.

Tucker killed Smith in self-defense, Tucker claimed, after he had found out his best friend was a vigilante cop.

Prior to this startling case, if there had been a bit of sanity in San Antonio's violent life, most local residents believed it had been the police department. If something went awry, then at least the police could help you out. Now, it looked like the police were part of the problem instead of the solution.

Overnight the deep trust the public placed in the department was gone. The police chief was fired. Department heads and deputy chiefs ran for cover. Some were reassigned and much of the top brass lost power. Heads rolled.

The police also instituted a wide variety of reforms in recruiting cadets and checking the mental welfare of its veteran officers to ensure another Smith-Tucker scenario never occurred again. And, as an attempt at a systemic solution to preserve and keep an accurate record at violent shooting scenes, the police also instituted a "shooting team" of specially designated officers who were charged with securing all of the evidence and investigating all shootings in which police were involved.

The Tucker-Smith case caused repercussions that weren't immediately fathomable at the time and certainly weren't understood by the local press, which turned on itself in a vicious feeding frenzy of accusations and counter accusations.

Besides that major scandal, other incidents occurred that served to remind many in the community that some police officers cannot be trusted and that others take themselves too seriously.

For example, in one, a Riverwalk barge captain was busy taking his band of hearty tourists on a float trip down the small canal the locals call the San Antonio River. As is usual on these trips, the captain began pointing out various local points of interest like the centuries old cedar tree on the river that stood during the Battle of The Alamo, the old watering hole where pioneers watered their horses, etc. At one point the young barge captain pointed to the side of the Riverwalk at some park rangers and said, "And there go our local park rangers. They're here to hassle you."

The boat rocked with laughter, until the park rangers made the barge pull over and the seventeen-year-old would-be comedian was arrested for disturbing the peace.

The tourists were irate. They knew the boy was joking, but apparently he didn't even know how much of a prophet he really was. I'd like to say the story has a happy ending, but it doesn't. The barge company fired the boat captain. They said he brought them bad publicity.

It's sad to say, but that type of thinking permeates life in San Antonio. Because, despite the violence, it can be a friendly sort of town—unless you happen to be in the wrong bar on the wrong street on the wrong night and someone's had too much to drink. The resulting chaos is referred to as a "misdemeanor murder." They occur almost every weekend in San Antonio—crimes of passion—they're also called, and it's easy to see how they occur once you understand San Antonio.

The police know and understand the town better than most. Each day they work the streets. Each night they arrest the drunks, the gang members, and the gun wielding vatos—or crazy guys.

That reality came crashing down on most of us at KMOL when one of our own staff members awoke one morning to find out a family member of his had been murdered.

Mike Guerrero was working as a part-time photographer in the Summer of 1989. He had joined us after working in a couple of other smaller markets. His desire had been to come home. In June, less than three months after Gary Williams died in that violent fight on the city's northside, Guerrero's closest relative, his baby sister, died in a macabre incident on the city's northwest side.

Roy and I were called in the midmorning hours of June 8th to a possible arson fire on Abe Lincoln Street. The police dispatcher said there might be a person trapped inside the house. Naturally this is the type of story television is interested in. We could get "really neat flame video" as our producer likes to remind us, and at the same time get some human drama on videotape too.

When I got to the address, I knew I had seen the place before. Just weeks earlier, Mike Guerrero had stopped here to say hello to his sister while we were out working on a story.

I grimaced at the recollection and hoped his sister wasn't inside, but soon the word was out: Judy Guerrero was inside. She had been tied up, shot in the back five times and the house set on fire to hide the gruesome murder. She was a pretty girl and no one in the neighborhood could say a bad thing about her.

But it says something that no one flinched over the details either—not the press and certainly not the public. Murders like this, while not everyday occurrences, seem to happen too frequently to puncture the callousness of the heart of the locals.

Mike, of course, heard about it. He drove up as the ambulance was preparing to bring the charred, shot-up remains of his sister out of the house.

I ran to him. I couldn't let his last memory of his closest relative be that of something that resembled overcooked barbecue. I quickly hustled him away.

"I can't believe it," he told me. "Not here. She was supposed to be safe here."

I knew what he meant. There is a common belief among San Antonians, that despite its melting pot charm, it is really a divided city. The eastside is supposed to be for the poor blacks, the Westside for the impoverished Hispanics, the Southside for the white rednecks and poor white trash, and the Northside is for those who've "made it."

If you live on the Northside (which encompasses the Northeast, North and Northwestern parts of San Antonio) as Mike's sister did, you're supposed to be safe. But "No one is immune to violence. You aren't safe anywhere in San Antonio if someone wants you bad enough," a police officer told me once. "You think you're safe living in Alamo Heights, or on the Northside, it's everywhere."

There is a revolving door syndrome in Texas' prisons. The average car thief is back on the streets in a matter of months, drug dealers spend about as much time in jail, and a cop killer was back on the streets less than ten years after he'd gunned down a San Antonio police officer in cold blood.

The judicial system is so bad, and the sentences criminals receive are so light because of overcrowded jails. I know several robbery and burglary detectives who've accurately been able to predict when the next crime spree will take place based on when the criminals in prison will be released and come back home.

And, most of the criminals do return home. They probably find the charms of San Antonio as hard to resist as the rest of the population.

After all, San Antonio has an international flavor that most other cities lack. There is its Mexican heritage, the Alamo, Sea World, and of course the River Walk. Springs and summers spent sipping icy marguerites underneath the shade of the towering, aging cedar and oak trees on the restaurants on the River Walk can easily lure one into a state of tranquility.

It's best not to look too close at your waiter or waitress though. They might be illegal aliens that came up with the Coyotes just weeks ago. Or perhaps they moonlight by selling cocaine or other drugs. San Antonio, being one of the largest cities near the Mexican border is a clearing house for all sorts of illegal drugs.

Maybe your waiter or waitress is only involved in using drugs recreationally and just shot up hours ago. Maybe they have no other source of income and are waiting tables to help feed the six or seven small mouths that wait in near poverty at one of the city's numerous housing projects.

It is in those projects, like the Alazon Apache

Courts on the near westside, that police have their greatest problems. Once, while shooting a special on the problems there, I ran across a fifteen-year-old boy. He was the father of a two-month-old son. He was out of work, out of school, and had no idea what he was going to do, although he said he wanted to marry his girlfriend so his son would have his name.

As I talked with him, I couldn't help but notice several large scars on him which had healed, and one fresh one that was still oozing pus. The gash went all the way across his right bicep and looked like it had struck bone. A piece of muscle was clearly visible.

"You've seen a doctor for that, I hope," I cautioned him.

"No."

"Why not?"

He shrugged, smiled and adjusted the black baseball cap on his head that identified which gang he belonged to. "Why should I? I didn't see the doctor for any of these others." And then he showed me even more scars he'd gotten in other knife fights.

After he left, the officer I was with turned to me. "We used to bust that kid's dad for child abuse and drug dealing before he got killed. His son's going the same way."

Roy, my partner-photographer, and I have seen too much of this.

Perhaps some salient statistics will explain why.

According to state records, there are twenty-seven thousand people on parole or probation in San Antonio and another twenty-seven to thirty thousand unserved felony warrants here: that's about five percent of the population wrapped up in that small part of the criminal justice system. It gives you a small idea of the problem some twelve hundred police officers face on a daily basis.

One of those cops facing the heat until he was killed, was Gary Williams.

Chapter 6

Subpoenas

The day after my interview with Henry Hernandez, I learned Dino Chiecchi was not the only one to question its validity. The *San Antonio Light* followed with an article that questioned whether I had really gotten the interview from Hernandez, and even if I had, the *Light* reporter went on to question whether I got the interview in jail, as claimed, or if I got the interview prior to Henry's arrest.

The *Light* erroneously reported that I had superimposed a photograph of the jail over the Hernandez interview inferring that the conversation took place in the jail. Actually, KMOL had superimposed Hernandez's photograph over the interview.

It was the beginning of a fishbowl existence for me and my family. For the first time, and definitely not the last, my credibility was questioned. My personality was examined and criticized. I was called "flamboyant," "obnoxious," and "arrogant" among others. Getting the Hernandez interview later proved to be as much a chance for the public to vote on my personality as my professional ethics. One of the people casting his voice was police Lieutenant Albert Ortiz.

Ortiz had taken over the police department's

homicide division after the Smith-Tucker scandal and had promised a professionally run department.

But, the city council had not been forthcoming with additional money for the department, and consequently he had fewer detectives in his division than he believed he needed. This was something that taxed him as an administrator since the number of murders in the city seemed to rise every year.

Albert was also involved in his own divorce. Like Gary Williams, he was ending a long-term relationship. Albert was having to juggle his personal life, administrative duties, and now the Gary Williams' case.

It was bad enough that another police officer had been gunned down in the line of duty, but the previous evening KMOL-TV had interviewed Henry Hernandez. What made it worse was that his own detectives hadn't talked with Hernandez. Now Albert was going to have to talk to me since I was the reporter who conducted the interview, and that was something he really wasn't looking forward to. He and Paul Buske had already visited KMOL-TV a few months previously when we'd tangled on another case, to talk with news director Ron Harig about my being an obnoxious, arrogant reporter. Now they were coming back with an even stronger complaint.

By Wednesday morning, Henry and Julian had been taken in leg irons to the jail's highest security area. The cells are located on the sixth and seventh floor in the Bexar County Jail and many of the bunks there are reserved for the members of the Mexican Mafia and Texas Syndicate—two notorious prison gangs. Among the inmates in the jail, it is widely known that to be admitted into the exclusive club on the jail's top floors, you must've committed a particularly gruesome act of violence—probably murder.

That same morning, Gerry Goldstein and Mark Stevens were making a couple of decisions that would affect the lives of all the key players in the Hernandez story for several years to come. Gerry had accepted, at the request of a Bexar County district court judge, a position as the court appointed attorney for Julian Hernandez.

This is the work that counts for Gerry.

"There is nothing we do as lawyers that is more important than defending a man who may loose his life," he said. "It's a very taxing prospect to be involved in a Capital Murder case, but it is our obligation to do that service to the community."

Gerry is known for his work with the American Civil Liberties Union and some say he is one of the best marijuana defense lawyers in the United States. Among his noted clientele is Dr. Hunter S. Thompson, a fellow Louisvillian of some renown.

Gerry was once described in a local newspaper as one of the flower children from the sixties who made good. His office on the twenty-ninth floor of one of the largest buildings looks out on the city. The hallway is decorated with that news clip and dozens of other framed memories from his many high-profile cases.

Gerry is the type that can smile at you, even as he sticks in the knife. He is also a master showman and one hell of a smooth operator. He once defended a police lieutenant on a drug charge and then publicly announced he would accept no payment.

"This man has given twenty-seven years to this community," Gerry announced. "This is my way of seeing that the community gives something back to him."

Diplomatic, meticulous, easy going, and deftly able to manipulate the law, Gerry is highly respected for his legal abilities and easily liked because of his charm.

Mark Stevens is also one of the best criminal defense attorneys in South Texas and used to work with Gerry. Some say he learned a lot from Gerry, except for diplomacy.

Mark is a fiery orator, a screamer, and some say a pit-bull dog in a courtroom. He's younger than Gerry, wears those round yuppie glasses that seem to be so popular, and has made a living out of ACLU cases and Capital Murder cases.

As he thought about the ramifications of the telephone interview with Henry Hernandez, Mark was enraged. He had been appointed by the court to handle Henry's case, and he wasn't thrilled that the attorney-client privilege had been negated and he was even less thrilled with the prospect that his client had confessed on a local news program.

He needed to talk with Joe Hernandez, the Hernandez family attorney who had handled the brothers' surrender and arraignment to see what had happened. In his mind, Mark made a mental note of all the constitutional violations that he felt had occurred when a KMOL reporter had interviewed his client.

How the hell did the press get to Henry?

Now, Wednesday morning, March 29th, was not an especially cloudy morning and it certainly wasn't dark at 7:30 A.M. when I got in my car to drive to work. Yet, it seemed as if every other car in traffic had its headlights on. I didn't understand why. Then, flipping through the FM radio stations, I found the explanation. A disc jockey was asking for a show of support from local residents for the police and in memory of Gary Williams. The response, gauged by what I saw as I drove into work, was phenomenal.

Arriving at the station shortly after 8 A.M., and despite the rigors of the previous day, I was ready to go, although I wasn't sure what the day would bring.

I had scarcely settled into my desk when a telephone call came in from Alvin "Rusty" Brown at the San Antonio Police Department's homicide division.

"We'd like you to come down and make a statement about the story you got." He seemed friendly enough and it was good to know someone had watched the news the night before.

"Rusty, I don't mind, but I'll tell you up front there were some confidences involved and I don't think I can betray them."

"I don't think we want to talk about it on the telephone, but I don't see any problem. We just need to take your statement. I'm busy this morning, can you come down tomorrow?"

I noted the appointment on my calendar, thanked Rusty for calling and then hung up the telephone.

Five minutes later a call came in from Gerry Goldstein's office. I had no idea why he would be calling me. I had interviewed him on a couple of gun control and marijuana stories, but I didn't know him all that well. In the back of my mind though I entertained the thought, as I picked up the telephone, that maybe he saw my story the night before and wanted to offer me his assistance.

No such luck. He was representing Julian Hernandez and while his office was calling, he sure wasn't. Cynthia Orr, his aide de camp talked to me, and she said she was warning me that I was about to be subpoenaed for all the audio tape and my notes from the interview.

I glanced at my watch. It was only nine A.M. and already I was in a fix and Ron Harig, our news director, wasn't in yet—just my luck.

I hung up the telephone and waited for whatever other little surprises were in store for me. To keep my mind occupied I feigned cleaning up my desk—a hearty task at the best of times and something I really shouldn't undertake unless I have two days of uninterrupted time staring me in the face.

Quickly giving up, I decided to call our station's attorney Larry Macon. I knew his number and figured he was going to have to get involved with this mess sooner or later. His receptionist told me he wasn't in either.

Suzanne Wolff, our managing editor at the time, was in so I went to talk with her. Suzanne is a small, feisty woman just under five feet tall. I don't think I've ever seen her without a cigarette sticking at an oblique angle out of her clenched lips, and I can't remember a time when she didn't remind me of a loaded and cocked pistol ready to go off—or perhaps a bulldog ready to bite. She has a gruff manner, but it covers a kind heart and a good manner—sometimes.

The little blonde tasmanian devil, as I called her, can't stand anything to do with the legal system and positively cringed when I told her what had happened that morning.

From inside her glassed-in cubicle, it probably looked like we were arguing—which wouldn't have been so unusual. I've often fought for and against stories and the managing editor is the one who has to wage those battles and negotiate truces with reporters.

"What exactly did they tell you," she said as she removed the omnipresent cigarette from her mouth and exhaled a cloud of noxious fumes.

"Just that they want the tapes and probably my notes and that they're going to send us over a subpoena."

"Who said that, the cops or Goldstein's office?"
"Both."
"Shit."
"Yeah," I echoed, "my thoughts exactly."
"Do you have any plans to do a follow-up story today?"
"Well, yeah. But I haven't had a chance to give it much thought. I'd like to try and get the dispatch tape and see what other fallout there is today, but I haven't really given it much thought."

Suzanne decided to play for time until she talked with Ron. "Well, go ahead and see what you can get on the story today. If any other attorneys or cops call you, direct them to me and we'll all get together with Ron later."

That was fine with me. I didn't relish the thought of fighting with attorneys all morning long.

"You got the tapes?" she asked as I got up to leave.

"I've got the production tapes in my desk. I don't know where the originals are. You want me to get them?"

"Well, see what's around. I don't want copies floating all over the newsroom. You might as well pull the scripts and make copies of them too."

"Sure."

I left her office, which is immediately adjacent to my desk and sat down at my work station. KMOL's newsroom is like most every other newsroom in the country—one big room with a bunch of dividers that offer reporters and anchors little privacy. The only folks who rate real office space are the news director, managing editor, and operation's manager. It's probably one of the little perks station management likes to extend to news management since the news managers don't get the big bucks the anchors do.

At any rate, I sat at my desk, scratched my head, ran through my notes from the previous night, and then decided to take a look at my script.

Retrieving the production tapes, I glanced at them, but didn't listen to them, and put them back in the desk. Finally, I decided to stop in at Buske's office and see, once again, if I could get a copy of the audio tape transmission between Gary Williams and his dispatcher, just prior to the shooting.

I knew as a matter of routine they would already have the audio tape from the dispatcher's last call to Gary Williams and I was very anxious to listen to it. Usually, a tape like that will tell you what call the officer was dispatched on and what his words were to his dispatcher or other officers.

Even though Buske had already told me of the department's intention to delay release of the tape, I walked into his office later that morning hoping cooler heads would prevail; he now had requests from every newspaper, radio and television station in town.

Of course, I had no such luck, but for a moment I thought I might get a break when Buske told me that Lieutenant Albert Ortiz, the head of the homicide division, wanted to talk to me.

This was a bit of a surprise, since Albert and I, at that point in time, did not get along very well. I thought him grim, ill-tempered, and plodding. I knew what he thought about me.

He sat in his office on March 29th, with the case file of one of the biggest murder cases his detectives would have to handle: the death of a fellow police officer.

He had about nine witness statements in the file, including those from the night watchman, the paper delivery man, and a few others who'd heard parts of the fatal confrontation between the Hernandez brothers and Gary Williams. He even had a witness who could testify that the white Mercury belonged to Henry Hernandez. But it really didn't amount to much. The case was weak, and everyone knew it.

Then came my interview. Albert had talked to dozens of people who had already volunteered copies of the tape from KMOL's ten o'clock news the previous night. It was good evidence, if he could use it, and Albert knew a lot of that would depend on me.

"So the television reporter finally got a scoop," he greeted me with that razor thin smile that you could mistake for jocularity if you didn't know Albert.

"Yes. I understand you want to talk to me."

He brought in detective James Holguin. Together they began to pump me for information. Albert began, "You're going to give us the raw audio tapes." I looked at Albert. He's short, balding and his head always looks shiny, as if he'd waxed it. But he has a way of being intimidating that's actually impressive and elusive to pinpoint. I knew he meant what he said more as a statement of fact, rather than a question.

"Sure, when you supply me with the dispatcher's tape," I replied. We both knew hell would freeze and I would be appointed police chief before that would happen. He dropped it. He said he had already received several copies of the videotape story I aired the previous evening, but that wasn't going to do. He wanted the raw tapes and probably everything else I had including my notes. I didn't seek any confrontations but told him it was probably going to be left in the hands of the lawyers because I had some sources to protect. He said that was fine, but I don't think he meant it. He wanted my material for a very important case and couldn't understand why I was standing in his way, unless, he thought, it was my ego.

Albert and I hadn't gotten along since the Jennifer Delgado case. Little seven-year-old Jennifer Delgado was stabbed to death while she and her mother were doing laundry at a west side laundromat in 1988.

I had been in town a little longer than a month. My wife was still in Kentucky and I was living in a home completely empty of furniture. I slept on the floor and ate delivery pizza almost exclusively since I had no refrigerator, stove, or food in the house. But that was okay with my dog, Jeremy, he didn't mind fishing through the boxes for pizza crumbs.

The day Jennifer got killed I was busy doing my laundry at a nearby laundromat when Joe Vesquez reached me on my pager. I called the station and found out they wanted me to cover the story of a little girl who'd been stabbed, coincidentally, as she and her mother had been doing their laundry.

Some unknown man had walked into the laundromat, deposited a quarter in a soda machine and when the machine failed to dispense a soda the young man became enraged, pulled out a pocket knife and stabbed the mother and the daughter. The mother went out into the street screaming for help as the assailant took off in a car. The little girl walked out into the street and seeing one of her friends cried, "Look at me, I'm bleeding!"

Parts of her intestine protruded from the ugly gash the knife had made. Jennifer collapsed in the street and died on the operating table hours later. The mother recovered physically, but never has emotionally. Along with her other children and her husband, Mrs. Delgado moved to the tiny town of Pearsall after she recovered from her knife wounds. Mrs. Delgado now resides with her husband and her remaining two children in a tiny, rusting trailer on an otherwise abandoned lot. A whole side of one of the trailer's walls is decorated with pictures of Jennifer, drawings she made for her mother and blue ribbons she won in academic contests.

At the scene of her murder, witnesses had seen part of a license plate on what was assumed to be the getaway car. The mother gave police a description that let to two vastly different drawings that were distributed around town. Rumors surfaced that maybe it was the mother's exboyfriend or someone else known to the family. On several occasions during news conferences, Ortiz had ducked our questions about his investigation. The Delgado murder was The Story in San Antonio for close to two months.

Finally, I got information that the police department had a suspect, had surrounded the man's home but somehow the man escaped.

Part of this was confirmed by an apartment manager who said a certain apartment had been surrounded, and yes, the police didn't arrest anyone, and yes, the tenant had checked out very quickly one night just prior to the police raid. The information was also confirmed by the neighbors and people who worked at the small convenience store across the street from the apartment.

I tried to set up an interview with Ortiz, telling him it was about an unrelated matter. He agreed. Then one of our own reporters at the station inadvertently tipped off homicide to what I was working on while she was talking to a sergeant in homicide about another story.

Seeing the story slug "Delgado Suspect" on the assignments board in the newsroom, she asked Sergeant Billy Ewell in homicide what the deal was. He didn't know and asked her what she was talking about. She said I was on my way over to talk to Lieutenant Albert Ortiz about the suspect they had in the Delgado murder. By the time I got to the police department Albert, I was told by Paul Buske, had left for the day and wouldn't be coming back.

"But I had an interview with him," I said.

"You lied about what the interview was about."

"So he left?"

"He isn't going to talk about the Delgado investigation. We've told you that and you refuse to believe it," Buske told me. "Lieutenant Ortiz has told me he won't ever do an interview with you again. You can't be trusted."

Well niceness didn't work, subterfuge didn't work. I finally resorted to the "ambush interview" tactic. If the police had blown one of the biggest murder investigations in the city, I wanted to know. So I waited until four thirty P.M. when I knew Albert Ortiz would walk out of the side entrance to the police department and make his way to his car and drive home.

Sure enough at the appointed time he walked out of the police station. I got out of my car with Roy, who had his camera rolling. I walked up to Lieutenant Ortiz to try and ask him a question. He had anticipated it. Quickly ducking into a car with Paul Buske, Buske looked at me, smiled and flashed me a sign that said "Three strikes. You're out!"

Jennifer Delgado's killer has never been found.

So, when I walked into Albert's office on March 29, 1989, there was a history we shared that wasn't too pleasant, and I was admittedly a little apprehensive about talking with him. I left his office feeling I'd accomplished little and wondered how Ortiz was going to handle the statement I'd soon give to Rusty Brown.

By midmorning Ron was talking with Bob Donohue, our station manager. Bob is a gregarious sort of guy with a Teddy Roosevelt aura about him. He's got the stuffed carcass of a bear he killed on a hunting trip lurking over an antique barber chair in his office. Next to the barber chair (the significance of which escapes me) is a framed picture of Bob with a bloody spear in his hand. The dead remains of a wild boar rest at his side. Once a fellow reporter at KMOL said that Bob's office looked like John Wayne's study. It probably does.

Bob was leaning on Ron to give up the tapes of the Hernandez interview.

"After all, it's a cop killer we're talking about here," Bob said. "The guy's a scumbag."

Ron tried to answer, but I interrupted. "I don't think that really has much to do with it. I don't think we should just turn over our raw tapes to the district attorney or anyone else. What we aired is the public record. Those raw tapes are like my notes."

Ron agreed in principle, but he told me, "This is a case that I don't think we should go to the wall for."

"You tend to see everything in black and white, Brian," he said. "Sometimes things aren't always like that. We have to balance the cost of going to court against what we would gain with the fight."

"Ron, I know that," I countered. "But I don't like being muscled by the district attorney."

"The defense is also asking for those tapes. If we fight this, we'll have no one on our side. It's a lopsided fight."

"Am I wrong to want to fight?"

"I didn't say that. But it's a fight that will be hard to win. Are you prepared to go to jail for this? It could end up that way, you know."

It was the first time anyone had put into words the worst-case scenario. It was always a dim thought in the back of my mind, but Ron had forced me to look at the possibility more clearly.

"What would you have me do Ron? I mean, if we

give in on this little thing, then it opens the flood gates. Every time we get something a lawyer wants, he'll feel like he can just waltz into our newsroom and take it. Doesn't that bug you?"

"Hell yes, it bugs me. But I'm not talking about the principle. I'm talking about what this station will have to go through, what the management will have to go through, and what you and Pam and the baby will have to go through."

"I know."

"And you know we also might take some hits on this. You're not the most popular person down at the courthouse."

"I know."

"Some see you as abrasive, obnoxious, arrogant . . ."

"Ron, I know all that, but like Donaldson said: You can call me obnoxious, you can call me arrogant, but when you want the job done right, you'll call me."

"Brian, you're not Sam Donaldson."

"Ron, I know. Look, I'm just trying to make a point. I know it will be difficult. I know it could get nasty. I know I could go to jail. But it's something I feel *that* strongly about. I don't think I'm wrong about this."

Our discussion ended a few decibels louder than it had begun. It was followed by a rather weighty silence as Ron stared at Bob and Bob looked at us both.

"We could give them the tapes and hope it makes them happy," Bob finally said.

"I'm inclined to agree," Ron countered. "Brian, what exactly is in your notes."

"Names, addresses and telephone numbers of people I used last night to get to Henry."

"Anything else?" Ron shot back.

"No. Joe transcribed the interview after master control got done cleaning up the tape for us, but we threw that stuff away last night." I was beginning to wonder what Ron had in mind.

He took a breath and mulled everything over for several minutes.

"Okay, Brian, when you speak to the police again tell them we're willing to entertain a subpoena for the broadcast tapes. If they ask for the raw, we'll take it from there after we talk to Macon. If they ask for the notes, we won't give them that."

Bob nodded, said that sounded like a game plan to him and he left. I remained in Ron's office and when it was clear, I closed the door.

"Ron, what do you mean 'if they ask for the raw?'" Ortiz already told me he wants the raw tapes and you can't give them the raw tape. You know the principle involved here." I was angry and frustrated.

"Yes. But as I told you before, that's not the only consideration."

"With me it is."

"I know. Why don't we wait and see what's in the subpoena. If we decide to give them the raw tapes we can always say it's an extraordinary circumstance and we give them the tapes because it's a capital murder case involving a police officer."

I left his office furious.

It boiled down to a principle. One that was important to me—the right of the press to protect its sources. I was still convinced that nothing my sources had to say would help or hinder the case. But that wasn't the point, either the freedom of the press was sacrosanct or it wasn't.

Ron was not buying all of it. He was willing to take the station off the hook by turning over the tapes the station had in its possession. At the same time he was strongly encouraging me to give up my notes and sources, because he didn't want to go to the wall. But, at the same time he said the station would back me. I was left, since I knew Ron's position, wondering how long and how far the station would go to make good on that promise.

There are few places for reporters to turn when they face a situation like the one I was in. I thumbed through a mental telephone list; The Freedom of Information Society, The Reporters Committee for Freedom of the Press, and Investigative Reporters and Editors.

By the time I reached my desk I had decided to call all of those organizations plus some attorneys. I started with I.R.E. because it is based at the University of Missouri, I went to school there and I know Steve Weinberg, the director.

Within forty-five minutes I'd gone through the entire list and the news wasn't encouraging. I had a tentative agreement from one local and one Dallas based attorney, should I need their services.

"Remember, when it's all said and done, the attorney you have right now is the station's attorney, not your attorney. He will have to protect the station's interest even before yours, if need be," one lawyer told me.

That was the good news.

The bad news was that I couldn't hang on to the tapes if the station wished to turn them over. Should those tapes contain any part of my conversation with Debra Ledesma or anyone else I wanted to protect, I could either erase the tape and face charges of destroying evidence, I could quit KMOL on principle or I could turn over the tapes.

"It boils down to this," one attorney told me. "Those tapes are essentially the property of KMOL-TV. They can do anything they want with them. If your news director decides to give them up, then you've got very little say in the matter."

That, as they say, was that. But, I figured if my station was going to give up the tapes, maybe I could get something in return—a trade of sorts. Earlier I had tried to be civil with Lieutenant Ortiz and Jimmy Holguin. Ron wanted me to call them back and tell them no tapes without a subpoena. What if I could get Holguin to trade me the dispatch tapes I so desperately wanted, for our tapes which they so desperately wanted? It seemed worth a try.

Picking up the telephone I called Holguin.

Jimmy, as always, was friendly.

I gave him Ron's name, told him what Ron told me to tell him and then tried to cozy up to him.

"You don't have your recorder on?" I asked knowing most homicide cops tape record all telephone conversations in their office. Jim assured me his recorder wasn't on.

"The two Hernandez brothers are animals, and the over-riding concern should be their prosecution," I said and tried hard to sound like I'd do what I could to cooperate with him.

It did me no good. All Holguin was interested in was getting my tapes without having to issue a subpoena, which I assured him was impossible. The only thing I was interested in was getting the dispatcher's tape without having to seek help from the Attorney General or a lawyer. That didn't happen either.

After I got off the telephone with Holguin, I again approached Ron Harig.

"Did you call the police department?" he asked.

"Yes I did. I also told them they could subpoena us for the tapes we've got left."

"Okay, we'll talk again later, after I talk to Larry Macon (the station's attorney)."

"All right. But, Ron I also tried to use our tapes to try and get the dispatch tape."

"The what?"

"The tape recording of Gary Williams talking to his dispatcher just before he died."

"Are we going to get it?"

"No. I don't think Holguin will budge on that. I tried to make it sound like I'd really like to help him, but he's only interested in our tape."

"Okay, we'll talk later."

My one attempt to get out of the debacle with even the smallest victory failed. What made matters worse was that Jim had not turned off his tape recorder either. That telephone conversation was my biggest mistake in the months I worked on the Hernandez story. It would come back to haunt me when I least expected it and when I was most vulnerable.

Chapter 7

A Funeral

The Castle Hills First Baptist Church sits in one of the quietly green parts of San Antonio more reminiscent of the Midwest than South Texas. The large stone building exudes a stoicism and dignity that makes one pass the building with head down in reverence.

Seven-hundred people gathered at the church Wednesday, March 29th, for Gary Williams' memorial service.

Most of the city's police brass were there, as were friends, family members, reporters and about one-hundred officers in full uniform.

The mottled sea of blue settled into their seats as two somber honor guard officers took their place beside Williams' flag-draped gun-metal gray casket.

Reverend George Harris, the church's pastor, broke the gloomy silence with words of praise for Gary and the police force. But perhaps what stuck with the audience most was a warning note that boomed across the church.

"Be aware of what you are—you are God's servants . . . be a good policeman like Gary was," he told the assembly.

"You need to be a man of integrity . . . and know

what you are not. You are not superhumans; you are not immune to the world of corruption and graft."

Grim, hushed faces filed out of the church on that cool Wednesday night to contemplate those words.

The next morning, Thursday, more than a thousand police officers showed up at the Mission Burial Park North as Gary Williams was laid to rest. Police from Houston, Dallas, Austin, El Paso, Laredo, and dozens of other cities in and outside of Texas formed a five-hundred-vehicle caravan that slowly wound its way through the city's streets to the cemetery.

Police Chief Bill Gibson took the opportunity to inform the media that he was not angry that the District Attorney had taken the Hernandez brothers into custody.

"The important thing is that they're off the street," he said. "But the idea that the Hernandez brothers were afraid to turn themselves in to the police because one of my officers might gun them down is ridiculous."

Sergeant Harold Flammia, who survived being shot five times by a burglar to become the head of the police union was even more direct.

"We don't have any more vigilantes left on this force," he said in an obvious reference to Stephen Smith.

The reporters nodded, the cameras recorded the event and we all waited as the long procession made its way past us.

"It kind of reminds me of Patty Calderon's funeral," Roy said to me.

I nodded in agreement and noted to myself that I'd seen too many funerals lately.

* * *

On Friday the subpoenas came.
Ron and I were hit with the exact same request:

> "The originals of any and all field and broadcast tapes, any and all audio recordings, any and all written or typed materials, any and all recorded information of any form concerning the shooting of S.A.P.D. officer Gary Williams and conversations with Henry D. Hernandez and/or Julian Hernandez by Brian Karam (sic) or any other representative concerning the death of S.A.P.D. officer Gary Williams for the period of March 27, 1989, to the present."

In more ways than Ron and I could fathom, we'd been had. He immediately got on the telephone to our lawyer, Larry Macon. According to him, the subpoena was opened ended. In other words, any story KMOL did on Gary Williams from March 27th to the day I died could be covered under the subpoena we held in our hands.

"Larry, what about this phrase 'any and all written materials'? Would my personal journal at home be covered under that?" I asked.

"Probably."

Larry calmed us down and told me the station would fight it.

"What about your statement to the police? Have you given it yet?" He added.

"No. I was getting ready to go down to the police department when the subpoena came."

"Well, I'll talk to Ron and you go down and give them the statement. If you have any questions, call me."

I thanked him and left Ron in his office talking with Larry on the speaker phone.

* * *

Detective Rusty Brown seemed genuinely happy to see me. He ushered me into his office and after a quick round of salutations we got to the heart of the matter. He asked me a few questions about what happened when I talked to Henry and then he asked me how I got the interview. Without going into specifics, I told him that I heard the brothers wanted to talk and I eventually obtained an interview. He typed everything up and presented a copy of the statement to me.

"You know none of us have talked to these two guys," he said.

"Yeah. I know Albert is kind of pissed that I got an interview with them."

"I don't want you to compromise any of your sources, but can you tell me how you got the interview. We can't touch these guys."

"Rusty, I'd love to but I can't."

"I understand. We have to work with confidences too." He paused for a moment, then added, "It wasn't anyone in the district attorney's office that helped you was it?"

For one of the few times in my life, I found myself at a loss for words. Before I could recover, Rusty spoke up again.

"I don't really want to know. I'm just curious because of all that nonsense in the papers and on television about how the D.A. had to protect the Hernandez brothers.

He tossed me a copy of one of the local papers. The headline read "Police upset at D.A." I quickly scanned the article. The story, dated Thursday, March 30th, quoted an unnamed "top-ranking police officer" who said district attorney Fred Rodriguez's handling of the surrender of the two Hernandez brothers was an insult to the police department.

A Funeral

"For the top law enforcement officer in Bexar County to make such a stupid statement that these two need protection is a personal attack on the Police Department," the senior officer said. "To say that a policeman would walk up to a suspect and kill him is ludicrous. That's saying the Police Department is not trustworthy."

I tossed the paper back to Rusty and thought carefully about what to say. There was an underlying tension between the D.A.'s office and the police department. The police felt the D.A. was too soft on many cases and the D.A. felt some police were too sloppy in their work. I didn't want to get involved in the politics between the two.

"Rusty, I can't tell you who helped me set it up, but I can assure you that this wasn't any kind of political ploy on the D.A.'s part to make you guys look bad. The idea to go after the interview was mine and the D.A. had nothing to do with it."

"That's all I wanted to know." He looked relieved.

I turned my attention back to my statement and wrote for a while. As I read it over I began to feel uncomfortable about a couple of references near the bottom of it. I asked to call Larry, and Rusty agreed. After I talked with Macon I turned back to Rusty.

"I'd just like to scratch out these two sentences. I think it makes references to how I got the interview that could cause me some problems."

He agreed to scratch them out. I initialed and signed the statement when he was done. Then I left.

By the time I got back to the station, the afternoon was gone. I walked into Ron's office.

"Are we going to give them the raw tapes?" As I asked this question I looked at Ron behind the desk. He was nervous and characteristically quiet.

"I talked to Larry. We might just try and give them the aircheck on a beta tape and see if that makes them happy. But, if they put up too much of a fight, we're going to give them the raw tapes as a fall-back position. That might avoid the larger fight over your notes," he said slowly.

I shook my head. "If you give them the raw tapes it's just going to make them think they can push us around and get anything they want from us, if they push us hard enough."

"Brian, we've already gone over this. The decision is final."

I left Ron's office without saying another word and gathered up my things to go home.

I was thinking very seriously about getting my own lawyer, fighting my own station, and probably losing my job in the prospect. I wondered if it was worth all the trouble.

Chapter 8

Searching for Evidence

We never got around to discussing the subpoena. I thought we should just try to quash the damn thing at the grand jury level. I was still convinced it was too broad. But, Ron and Larry decided on a middle ground. We would appear at the grand jury and give them the tape of the story that aired on March 28th and we would provide them a script. The story was to be recorded on a high-speed, broadcast quality beta tape and we knew beforehand the county had no way of viewing it.

But Larry and Ron hoped, that by the time the attorneys got around to knowing they couldn't play the tape and by the time they actually needed it, the tapes might be a moot point.

"With any luck," Larry explained, "No one will ever have to go to court."

I kept my mouth shut. Having grown up in a family of attorneys, I couldn't believe it would work. I was sure we'd be pounced on by the grand jury.

* * *

I felt kind of sneaky as we walked into the grand jury room. A young assistant district attorney took the tape and script, "Is that all you're supposed to give me?" she asked.

"That's everything KMOL will provide," Larry said earnestly.

She didn't even blink. She excused us. We left.

I couldn't believe it would be that easy, or could it?

"That's it?" I asked Larry. We gave the court no notes, no raw tapes and the assistant didn't even realize Larry had answered her question in the negative. Best of all I didn't have to go on the witness stand.

"It ain't over with yet," Larry whispered. "That wasn't the attorney prosecuting the case. Beth Taylor is going to be the prosecutor and she's out on another case. You can bet she'll look a little closer at that tape then her assistant did."

Again, I wondered why we were pursuing a strategy that seemed only to postpone the inevitable. But, I walked along in sullen silence and kept my mouth shut.

When I got back to the station I called Steve Weinberg at I.R.E. and Jane Kirtley at the Reporters Committee for the Freedom of the Press, and the lawyers I'd talked to earlier when I'd thought about outside representation.

They all told me that as I outlined the facts they would have handled things "a little differently" than Larry, but they also added that they didn't know all the facts and that Larry and KMOL's actions didn't seem unreasonable.

I was ambivalent. I had already resolved myself to a court battle, and if it had to come I wanted to do it and get it over with. The court would never get my sources without a ruling; it was that simple.

But, if Ron and Larry could postpone the court battles long enough that the fight for my notes would be dropped, then that would be okay too.

The stress was beginning to get to me. I knew I'd have to get a better grip on myself if this thing were to linger on.

The next day, the *San Antonio Light's* story noted that I had been subpoenaed to "reveal a source who helped set up an exclusive interview with an accused police murderer that aired March 28—the day of the arrest."

It further noted that "Karem said the station Wednesday turned over the televised interview and script."

Meanwhile, the police were having troubles of their own. By the first part of April, they still hadn't found Gary Williams' gun. On the last day of March, the police sent forty-three members of a police cadet class out to the crime scene where they scoured the area searching for more clues.

En masse they searched diligently, and were quite a sight to see from the highway, but they found nothing.

Greg Trimble, a private detective, took all of the Gary Williams' news in much the same way as the rest of the city did. He felt sorry for the officer, probably more so than others since he had roots in law enforcement, and he hoped the killers would be brought to justice.

Trimble has been a stalwart in the local democratic machine, providing much of the unglamorous grunt work needed by political candidates.

Greg got a call from Mark Stevens just a few short days after the Gary Williams murder. Mark wanted

Greg to go to work for him as an investigator for Henry Hernandez.

He balked. "I've been with law enforcement all my life," the amiable private detective with the salt and pepper hair and perpetual tan commented. "There's no way I want to get involved in that!"

But Mark can be persuasive: so Greg agreed to make a trip over to the jail and visit with Henry. Even days after being arrested, Greg could see how tired and ragged Henry looked.

"Are you well?" he asked Henry.

"All right. How's my family?" was Henry's first question.

As they talked, Greg was impressed with Henry's quiet demeanor and concern for his family. Greg finished the interview equally impressed with what he was told about Julian. Leaving the visitation booth Greg tracked down Alex Ramirez.

"What do you mean letting the press interview our client?"

Alex, who was standing at the front of the jail, was temporarily taken back.

"What do you mean?"

"I'm working for Henry Hernandez and somebody in this jail let a reporter talk to him. Don't let it happen again."

With that, Greg stalked off, leaving Alex speechless. Greg's next stop was to let Mark Stevens know he would take the case.

By the second week of April, life had settled into a very dull routine for both Henry and Julian, although it was a quite different routine.

Jail Administrator Tom Barry had the brothers living in different parts of the jail and had heard of no problems with either one of them. But guards who had befriended and gotten to know Henry and Julian had noticed a big difference between the two. Julian, who was also accused of Capital Murder followed the rules, worked hard at his first assigned job cleaning up floors, and was then allowed out of his prison cell area to work in the cafeteria.

Meanwhile, it was reported that Henry was seen making friends with some fellow inmates who were career criminals.

"There's a dark side to Henry," one of the jail guards told me. "It's like he's given up on everything."

On April 13th, police recovered Gary Williams' gun. A South Side man turned it over to police by calling Crime Stoppers. He told police officers that a friend of his had found it soon after the shooting.

The next day Julian's attorney, Gerry Goldstein, Henry's attorney, Mark Stevens, and the prosecutor reached an agreement with the judge about bond. Judge James Barlow set the bond at $250,000 for Henry and $100,000 for Julian. Henry got the heavier burden since our story had him pegging himself as the trigger man.

District Attorney Fred Rodriguez said he would have preferred the two brothers were held without bond, but he was satisfied.

"With the compromise, I avoided at least two hearings . . ." he said. "Plus I don't think they'll be able to make it (the bond)."

Rodriguez grinned. He was coming up for reelection and nothing looks better for a reelection bid than nailing cop killers.

By this time Judge Barlow, now aware that we hadn't turned over the raw audio tape, "ordered KMOL to turn it over immediately."

When I got the word that day that our little attempt at subterfuge had failed, I was disappointed. I knew a showdown was looming—soon.

Many of us in the newsroom were finding the events too strange to believe.

"How can an interview a reporter obtained be admissible in court?" Dave Roderick asked me.

The red haired Roderick had been at KMOL for about three years at the time and was considered one of the most solid local television journalists. He occasionally wrote opinion pieces for the *San Antonio Light* and seemed far too literate to be involved in television. His arid sense of humor set him apart from others. But he was dead serious about the prosecution and the defense's desires to have my notes, sources, and tape.

"I just can't believe it."

"Neither can I, Dave." Our cubicals sat caddy-corner from each other in the newsroom. "I just wish the judge would see it our way."

"They have to. I can't believe he'd let that nonsense go on for long."

I couldn't give the matter much more thought. I was too busy trying to follow up on my original story about Hernandez's and Williams' fatal confrontation. First, I needed to find the guy Henry had supposedly stabbed which led to Henry's previous attempted murder charge, and in that way find out about Henry's past. Second, I needed to contact Henry's cousin—to see to what lengths I was supposed to go to protect her. Third, I needed to find out more about Williams' background. It was here that I was having the most trouble: many of the officers I knew that worked with Williams described him as a quiet, unassuming fellow who got along real well with other officers. No one, it seemed, knew much about him, or if they did they simply weren't talking. It seemed strange and I marked that fact down to be checked on later.

But, my first task remained my immediate concern, and I wasn't having any luck. The district attorney's office informed me that Leroy Chavez, the man who claimed Henry Hernandez stabbed him, had disappeared. Police and the district attorney's office said he didn't want to testify against Hernandez.

Chapter 9

Court Battles

Beth Taylor is a bitch.

Don't take my word for it. She has a poster hanging in her office which declares her so and Beth has been known to proudly declare herself as such.

It is a mistake, though, to think her pit-bulldog image is all there is to the woman. She is also perhaps the toughest prosecutor to work in the Bexar County District Attorney's office in at least the last twenty years. She has worked in several capacities with the Bexar District Attorney's office for the last sixteen years and has handled felony trials since 1977.

She would be the lead attorney for the state in the Henry and Julian Hernandez case. It was her fourth capital murder case.

Beth is thirtish and nearsighted. This is augmented by her omnipresent stylish eyeglasses that also seem to magnify her eyes.

Defendants, their witnesses and even a few prosection witnesses have withered under her stare. Because, although not many would call Beth Taylor a tremendous beauty, she can mesmerize you with those eyes. Then, once lulled into a sense of well being, she'll lash out at you with a steel edged voice that cuts right through you.

Inside her office at the Court House, her soft side shows at first glance. There is usually a Mozart tape playing on her small cassette player. The office, one assistant district attorney once said, looks like a yuppie's paradise. There are small house plants scattered across the room. Wall hangings of cats, small cat statues, and other items bespeaking the virtues of the domesticated feline are also a central part of the digs.

Beth's obsession with cats once got her into a minor problem when the county janitors found she was harboring several strays in a box under her desk. She couldn't understand the furor and wondered why people didn't treat animals kinder. Of course, she apologized and gave the kittens good homes.

Besides the cat paraphernalia, Beth also has a coffee maker available in her office, which has been known to produce some exotic types of coffee and tea for friends, acquaintances, witnesses, and anyone else who wanders by.

All of this, including Beth's attire, which is straight out of an episode of *thirtysomething*, can throw you off guard about the woman—that is until you notice the small sign on her desk which proclaims how proud the dweller of the office is of being called a bitch.

Detectives, fellow prosecutors, defense attorneys, reporters, and just about everyone who has ever met Beth has at one time or another called her or thought of her as a bitch—but use that term with respect.

"She can intimidate just about anybody," Lieutenant Albert Ortiz once said of her. "She's the best prosecutor this county's got."

Beth, though, has done her fair share of intimidating, which is partially responsible for her endearing nickname.

The other reason for her nickname is her dedication which some say is obsessive to justice. "I have a duty, and this may sound corny to some—to seek justice," she once said in federal court. It would be corny said by most, and maybe with her at the time as well, but she remains an idealist; she believes in the American judicial system.

This overriding sense of justice has sometimes led her to use her sharp tongue to carve up her own witnesses. For instance, top police brass felt the acid sting of her bite when she dressed them down after a homicide detective perjured himself on the witness stand on a high profile San Antonio murder case which made the D.A. and the police look like fools.

Beth Taylor does not suffer fools gladly. By nature she shuns the press, thinking reporters to be a thorn in the side of the justice system, so she had little reason to know who I or Ron Harig was—or care. But she did know the subpoena that had been issued to me and KMOL-TV had not been honored. She couldn't even play the tape KMOL had supplied her, and other than the tape all she had was a transcript of the broadcast story. Surely reporters kept notes? She was more than a little frustrated and slightly angry.

She had been busy the day the grand jury met to take our testimony, or perhaps she would have found out sooner. But things would come to a head soon enough.

On Friday, April 14th, the day after a man called Crime Stoppers and turned in Gary Williams' missing service revolver, Larry Macon and Ron Harig made KMOL's first appearance in court.

Larry Macon had talked to us previously about

his strategy, and now once again reinforced his promise to try and quash the State's and defense attorneys' subpoenas calling for my notes and raw audio tape of the Henry Hernandez interview on First Amendment grounds.

If he was successful on this point, I might never need to appear in court. Ron, as the head of the newsroom, was the legal guardian of the raw audio tapes and everything else concerning the Hernandez stories —except my notes. Larry decided Ron would first go to court to try and head off any probing into the area of sources and notes. Larry knew where I stood on that. Stoic, calm, rational, and unerringly professional in his demeanor, Ron was considered the best witness to take to court to try and diffuse the bomb that threatened to send me to jail.

But, by going to court, and as the legal custodian of KMOL's newsroom records, Ron also faced the possibility of going to jail himself. So, even though Ron had never thought this to be a fight he wanted to go the distance on, he would now face the heat on the witness stand. He would have to explain newsroom operations in depth, and would be queried as to why KMOL had not fully complied with the subpoenas.

The hearing took place at the old Bexar County Courthouse in the same chambers where the Hernandez brothers had been magistrated just a few weeks earlier.

Since I was not expected to be called on in the opening rounds of the questioning, I did not got to the hearing. Ron and Larry had me on standby in case they needed me, but I was expected to go about my daily duties. Larry said I had nothing to worry about at this stage.

Inside the courtroom, though, Larry and Ron did some worrying. Both tried to implement the strategy they'd discussed before the hearing, but they weren't having much success.

"Would you explain the differences between the tape that appeared on TV and the out-takes?" Larry asked Ron.

"The tape that appeared on television is the edited story that we broadcast, or stories in this case. This is every story directly related to the incident. These are the stories that we broadcast.

"We edit from raw material that is much like the television equivalent of our notes. After these stories are edited the raw material is not generally kept. Sometimes we'll keep it for a period of days. Other times the tapes are simply used again and recycled," Ron answered in his no-nonsense monotone, "We consider material that we routinely don't keep or consider part of the story—our raw material, our notes or unprocessed material. We don't consider it part of our finished product, part of our final report."

Larry broke in in his high pitched, angst filled voice. "Do you consider that privileged under the First Amendment?"

"Yeah."

"I'll pass the witness." Larry had made his point and stopped.

But Mark Stevens, Beth Taylor, and Gerry Goldstein weren't going to let that be the final word.

Mark took the first crack. "Have you seen both the stories that were aired as well as the outtakes?" he asked.

"No," came Ron's reply.

"So you haven't even seen the outtakes that you're claiming a First Amendment privilege about?"

"We tend not to routinely view outtakes," Ron said in a deadpan. He was right too. In most major news organizations few people have the time, inclination, or need to look at video that doesn't make the air. One exception to the rule are those who look for blooper video for the station's Christmas party. The most compelling exception, though, according to other news directors I know, is when your newsroom does a story that lands you in court.

Mark and the other attorneys apparently thought the facts surrounding the Hernandez case merited at least a casual viewing from the news director.

Mark hit Ron again. "So the answer to my question is, you personally, you're claiming a First Amendment privilege about something you've never even seen?" Mark asked.

"That's correct," came Ron's calm reply.

"So you don't claim that there are any secret conversations on those outtakes do you?" Mark was now trying to get into the territory of my notes and sources, a subject he had to know very well, since Henry was his client.

"No," Ron answered. Not having the pleasure of listening to, or viewing the outtakes he did not know what was on them.

But, again many news directors will also say, this isn't unusual. Any given television story may take up to anywhere from a half an hour to five hours of video tape. There may be a dozen or more stories shot on any given day. If a news director routinely reviewed raw tapes he would never do anything else.

Having exhausted that line of questioning, Gerry Goldstein stepped up to take his turn at hammering Ron; trying to discredit not only his managerial ability, but his wisdom in pursuing a course of action that would keep those tapes from the defense and prosecution.

"You have refused to provide those [tapes] to the defense under both Mr. Stevens request, on behalf of

Henry Hernandez, and myself, on behalf of Julian Hernandez, the outtakes," Gerry said in his best orator's voice. "Is that correct?"

"We have requested that the material that we broadcast be accepted as part of the public record," Ron said as he tried to dodge the implications that we had not fully complied with the subpoena.

"And a corollary to that," Gerry continued, "is that you are resisting the subpoena for the outtakes?" He now had Ron cornered.

"We are asking the court to understand our position."

"And your position is that you don't want to give us the outtakes?"

There was a slight pause before Ron answered, "We prefer not to."

Beth Taylor drove the final nail in our coffin when she got up and questioned Ron. Not content with dancing around any matter, Beth made her usual viciously blunt lunge at Ron's quivering jugular.

"So you did not therefore, comply fully with the grand jury subpoena, did you?" she asked Ron.

"No, we did not." Ron can be equally blunt. Although as is in character for the man, he did not raise his voice above a conversational tone.

Now, all three attorneys had seemingly succeeded in showing that KMOL had little regard for subpoenas —a grand view to have if you're a journalist, but a hideous view to display to a judge. Things were looking bleak for the KMOL team and it only got worse.

Mark Stevens took the opportunity to ask Ron how I had the opportunity to talk to Henry Hernandez and just how close I'd been to his client. Henry Hernandez was under the misconception that I, and not Alex, had passed the yellow post-it note with KMOL's

Court Battles

telephone number on it to him, and Mark was understandably furious.

"Were there any face-to-face conversations, as far as you know?" Mark angrily asked.

"Not that were recorded," Ron said slowly. "I think there was a face-to-face contact during the booking process or the arraignment process." Ron was referring to the media event at the courthouse where I and dozens of other reporters witnessed Henry and Julian walk to and from Barlow's courtroom. But, Mark had mistaken Ron's answer for something he thought was more horrifying.

"At the jail?" Mark was incredulous. Could it be that the Sheriff had actually allowed a reporter inside the Bexar County Jail to solicit an interview with a Capital Murder suspect while that suspect was being booked into jail?

"I think there was some contact there," Ron calmly replied. Evidently Ron mistakenly assumed that the media event I'd attended occurred at the jail.

Mark pressed the point. "You think there was some contact at the Bexar County Jail between Henry David Hernandez and your reporter, face-to-face?"

Ron's face was grim. "There was an attempt to have a conversation. I don't know how much conversation was had." Ron was at least consistent, if not accurate.

However, his answer was damaging to my credibility; the attorneys and judge handling the Hernandez case now saw me as an unprofessional manipulator who had taken unbelievable advantage of a perceived leadership problem at the jail. Ron's answer also scuttled our chances of quashing the subpoenas on First Amendment or any other grounds. No judge in the world wants to support someone who openly defies a subpoena, no matter how right or wrong that subpoena is. But now Barlow also had to deal with what seemed to be a reporter flaunting the rules so flagrantly that he was able to waltz into the Bexar County jail and talk face-to-face with an inmate who'd just been arrested for killing a cop.

Judge Barlow somberly announced he wanted KMOL to turn over to the court every shred of evidence we had about the Hernandez brothers.

Then he asked Larry Macon if he still wanted to fight turning over the tapes to the nice attorneys who wanted it for their case. Macon said he did.

Barlow's face tightened, "I'm going to refuse to quash the subpoena. I'm going to order you to produce all conversations between the man in jail that you have recorded and the reporter." Barlow's decision was a deep blow. But, Larry could appeal the decision. Of course, refusing to turn over the tapes while appealing Barlow's decision would put Ron in a position where he could be cited with contempt of court and thrown in jail since he was the guardian of those tapes.

He paused, a heavy silence filled the air. Larry and Ron had a few moments to mull over all the possibilities; then the judge turned and looked at Ron.

"When can you produce it?" Barlow asked Ron.

"Would a written transcript . . ." Ron ventured.

Gerry Goldstein quickly jumped in, "No."

"They want the tapes," Barlow said.

Now it was decision time. How would the station stand up to the principle Larry had defended just moments before? Would they open Ron to a contempt charge and jail?

Larry looked at Ron. "Tuesday?"

"We could certainly try." Ron answered hesitantly.

The tapes would be turned over to the State. But,

the attorneys weren't done with it yet. Goldstein, the grinning cheshire of an attorney as Hunter Thompson likes to describe him, tossed in this:

"Your Honor, the subpoena; it appears that there may have been an in-person interview as well, which may contain his notes of that interview . . ."

Picking up on Ron's mistake, Goldstein was now hot after my notes since he and everyone else now believed I had conducted an in-person interview with Henry Hernandez the day he was booked into jail.

The stage was set for round two. I was told to appear in court May tenth.

In the interim I tried to continue my pursuit of the Hernandez story.

Chapter 10

Leads and Deadends

On Friday, April 21st, 1989 I got in touch with a police officer on the West Side who knew the Hernandez brothers and Leroy Chavez. He told me of a restaurant near the new County Jail where the Hernandez brothers, Chavez, and others hung out.

Friday afternoon I got permission from the assignment desk to spend the day working on the story. Roy and I, dressed in jeans and T-shirts, drove over to the restaurant, and began talking with the patrons. None of them knew the Hernandez brothers or Chavez. But, a tall Hispanic man who worked behind the counter did.

The man called himself Raul, or Ruley. Most of our conversation took place in a language known as "Tex-Mex," a bastardization of English and Spanish indigenous to most of the border areas in Texas. Raul told me that Chavez had been in the restaurant about a week ago and had left in a black cab about midnight. Raul didn't remember the name of the cab company. He did remember seeing Henry Hernandez about a month ago at the restaurant—that made it just before Henry was involved in shooting Gary Williams.

"Where did Henry go when he left here?" I asked.

"No se. Hey vato, I don't watch that guy. You go to the Alazan if you want him."

"The Apache Courts?"

"Yeah. You know another?"

"No. I didn't think he lived there."

"Hey, man, I just said that's where to find him."

I thanked the man, suddenly realizing the significance of what he was saying. Roy and I walked out the front door.

"Where to now, partner?" He asked.

"Well, we have to find out which cab Leroy took first. I need to talk to that guy. Then, we have to find out what Henry was doing at the Alazan Apache Courts."

We got into the car.

"I think I know which cab company the guy was talking about," Roy said. "There's a company that uses black cabs not too far from here. It's over by the station. We can check."

That sounded fine by me, so we took off to only Roy knew where. I had planned to check some cab companies in the phone book, but if Roy had a hunch, why not play it. He grew up in San Antonio and I'd learned to trust his judgment in these matters.

A few minutes later, we pulled up to the cab company. I got out with Roy and we went inside where I asked to see the manager. An old man with a graying beard approached us with one of those universal red, oily rags that car repair people use. It was hanging from his front pocket. He picked it up and wiped his equally oily face with it.

"Whatcha need? What can I do for you?" He coughed as he spoke trying to clear his phlegm laden throat.

"I'm trying to find out if any of your drivers

picked up a fare at a restaurant by the jail last Friday around midnight." I gave him the address.

"You a cop?"

"No. I'm a reporter for KMOL-TV."

"Oh yeah." He coughed again, his words came out in small gasps. "I watch KENS. I love Debora Knapp Bonilla. Cute girl."

"Yes sir. That's nice."

"I like Lori Tucker too, but Debora I met only once."

It never ceases to amaze me why people watch our news, or don't. Anyway, I made small talk with the man for a few moments while he fumbled through his log book. Finally, he came across the Friday entries.

"No. We didn't pick up anybody like that last Friday."

I thought for a second. Raul hadn't specifically said Friday. I asked the manager to check the rest of last week, if he could. He did. The entry I needed was on Wednesday. A cab driver had picked up a fare at the restaurant at 11:38 P.M. and had taken him to an address on the East Side.

I thanked the manager and asked him if I could talk to the driver who picked up the passenger. I had to wait, because the driver was out on a run and should be back soon.

Roy and I talked outside while we waited.

"What do you want to talk to the driver for? We got the address. Let's go. We're wasting time." Roy said.

"No. Let's just wait. This guy might be able to tell us something." Roy was anxious to wrap this up. It was close to three P.M. and he got off at five. He doesn't like to put in overtime without good cause and right now we had nothing on tape. In Roy's opinion, that meant we weren't spending our time on a good cause.

The driver came a few minutes later and told us that he remembered the fare. The man who had called for his cab that night had long hair, a dark complexion, and spoke with a noticeable Hispanic accent. Great, I thought, that narrowed it down to about half the population of San Antonio. The driver didn't remember his passenger's name, but told us that he did remember that the guy acted like he was scared—of what, the cab driver couldn't say.

By late that afternoon, sometime before 4 p.m., Roy and I made it to the East Side address the cab company had provided us. We got out of the car and I walked up to a gray and white sideboard house with a glassed in porch. I rang the bell and then knocked. After a few minutes, a tissue skinned old woman opened the door just a crack. I could see the chain on the door which kept her from opening it any more.

"What do you want," came this scratchy voice.

"Excuse me, ma'am, I hate to bother you, but is Leroy here?"

"Who are you?"

"My name is Brian Karem. I work for Channel Four news."

"Do you have some identification?"

"Yes, ma'am." I held up my Texas Department of Public Safety press pass. It's official looking, issued by the State and means almost nothing.

She looked at it and then said, "There's no one here by that name."

I wasn't sure what she meant by that.

"I'm sorry, ma'am, but does that mean he lives here and isn't here now, or that no one by that name lives here?"

She slammed the door shut. So much for that. Roy and I walked back to the car. It looked to me like a dead end.

"You know," said Roy. "If he was scared, maybe he didn't have the cab driver drop him off at his house. He might live somewhere around here, but not here."

"That's great, where do we start? I mean, what do you want to do, knock on every door in the neighborhood?"

"No."

We got into the car, but before we could drive away, I thought about it. Roy was right. If the guy were a friend or acquaintance of Henry's, chances were he couldn't afford a house like the one I just visited anyway. He probably couldn't afford much at all. I looked across the street at the small, rundown apartment complex that looked like one of those motels that charge hourly rates. There were only about a dozen apartments to check, so again I figured why not, it was worth a shot.

We got back out of the car and checked the labels on the mailbox. Not one of the twelve boxes had any names on them. Great. So now we were reduced to knocking on doors.

After I knocked on the first door and got no response, a man walked out of an apartment on the second floor. "They're not there. Chuey and his old lady went to the store," the man told me from the top of the steps.

"I'm looking for a guy named Leroy," I told him. "Anybody by that name live here?"

I saw him glance at Roy's camera and our KMOL-TV van.

"He lives over there," he pointed at an apartment. "But you didn't get that from me." He hurried back inside.

At number six, a first floor corner apartment, a small demure woman with a baby boy in her arms answered the door.

"Hi, is Leroy here," I asked.

"No. He's at work right now. Who are you?" The woman asked me very quietly.

"Wait a minute," I stopped her. "Leroy Chavez, he lives here?"

"Yes. Who are you? A cop?" I thought my occupation would seem immediately obvious since Roy was lurking in the background with a big television camera on his shoulder. But maybe she just wanted to be sure.

"No. I'm Brian Karem, I work for Channel Four news. I'd like to talk to him about Henry Hernandez."

"I don't know if he wants to talk about him. Henry killed his brother."

"He did? I thought Henry stabbed Leroy."

"He did that too. Henry kills everybody who doesn't do what he says."

"Really? This the same Henry Hernandez that's in jail for killing the cop?"

"Yes sir. He's the same one that has everybody scared of him. He's not a nice person. Talk to the people at the Alazan Apache Courts. They can tell you."

This was the second person who'd referred me to the Courts. The Alazan is a fifty-year-old housing project on the West Side that's famous for drug dealing, drive-by shootings, and gang activity. It's home for a lot of the Mexican Mafia gangsters. The homeboys may be safe there, but it's not a place to go wandering through after dark—and sometimes not during the day.

Once, I had to go to the Courts following a couple of months of bloodshed there. The Mexican Mafia was having a power struggle and leaders ordered, and had their soldiers carry out, the execution of several of their members who found themselves on the wrong side of the powerful. For a five o'clock live shot I had to stand in the Courts and make reference to this violence.

I set up the live-truck, looking over at some vatos sitting in the shade of one of the apartments, and watching them bring a shot-gun and a hand gun out onto the porch. They looked at me and smiled. I smiled back and waved. They laughed. I did my live-shot and then got out of there very quickly.

Roy and I asked the woman when her husband, Leroy, got home and she said sometime after five. She didn't have a telephone, but we asked her if we could stop by on Monday and talk with her husband. She said it would be okay, because he didn't work on Mondays. I asked her if she knew what her husband was still afraid of since Henry was in jail. She told me Henry had threatened her husband again and he wasn't taking any chances.

We thanked her and left. Luck had been with us. Tracking down the slimmest of leads, we'd found Leroy, and if our luck held we could interview him.

Our last stop, before we called it quits for the day was to the Alazan Apache Courts. Several policemen who worked there told us Henry was well known to them. He was a two-bit drug dealer and violent type who'd been arrested several times. It seemed, according to these officers, that he had been trying to organize some sort of gang when he had killed Gary Williams. They gave me the names of several people in the Courts I could talk to.

It was close to five, but Roy said he would stick with it.

"This is getting good," he told me, temporarily forgetting his edict that no story is worth spending overtime on unless he's shot video for it.

We talked with several people, but no one wanted to go on camera. They told us Henry was so violent they were sure he'd find some way to get at them even though he was in jail. This is the typical attitude of those who live in the Courts and aren't involved in the drug or random violence trade—which is a majority of residents there. They've been so terrorized, so victimized, that they're scared to say or do anything that would bring the wrath of the violence peddlers down on them any more.

Life in the housing projects, one official with the San Antonio Housing Authority told me, is a lot like the state motto of Kentucky: "United We Stand, Divided We Fall." The drug dealers and gangsters are so good at dividing and conquering those poor victimized souls in the Courts, that those people never realize they're in the majority. If they simply took a collective breath, I have also been told, those who live in the projects could shake off the gangsters like so many dead fleas.

Roy and I retired for the weekend. We had nothing on tape, but a lot of information that I was sure we could turn into a decent story on Monday. We did.

Monday morning we talked with Leroy Chavez. He showed us five different scars on his back and chest that he said Henry Hernandez gave him in a fit of rage, because Leroy wouldn't deal drugs for him.

"Why didn't you press charges? Why didn't you show up in court?" I asked him.

"I told the police I wanted to press charges when I was in the hospital. They took down my name and address but no one ever contacted me when I got out of the hospital. He killed my brother and I want him to pay."

"Why did he kill your brother? How?"

"He stabbed him and stabbed him. He wanted to

get even because my brother was helping me. Henry is crazy. He will kill you for no motive. For no motive."

Leroy was nervous, sweaty, and quite convincing. Either he was a man who'd missed his calling as an actor, or he was genuinely afraid of the very same quiet, polite Henry Hernandez I'd met, who now stood accused of killing a police officer.

We wrapped up the interview and then headed over to the courthouse to talk to the district attorney who handled the prosecution of Henry's case. We caught Fernando Ramos outside a courtroom during a lunch break.

Fernando isn't very tall and has a swarthy appearance that I've often thought must make him a hard sell before a jury. He was in a very big hurry, he told me, but could spare just a moment if we were going to interview him on camera.

Naturally Roy and I obliged. We had no sooner set up the camera, than Fernando told me he had wanted to prosecute Henry Hernandez, but just never got the chance.

"Don't you realize that if you'd been successful in prosecuting this guy, he couldn't have been on the streets this March when he shot Gary Williams?" I asked.

"Yes, but we could never find Leroy Chavez. He was afraid to testify. We couldn't find him . . ."

"I found him."

"We could not. What can I say?"

I shook my head and left. Chavez had said he wanted to testify. Ramos, in the district attorney's office, said Chavez didn't and that Chavez couldn't be found.

"Hijo!" Roy exclaimed. "We got him. We found Chavez in less than a day!"

"Yeah, and we can't even use a subpoena."

"That's gonna make the D.A. look bad, man," Roy countered. "Hijo! That's real bad. Ramos looked like a fool."

During KMOL's afternoon story conference I outlined how Roy and I had found Chavez, and told Ron and our ten P.M. producer, Linda Lupatkin, what our plans were for a story that night.

"Do you know whether or not this would have meant Henry could have been kept off the street?" Linda asked. "You know what I mean? If they'd gotten a conviction, Henry wouldn't have been on the streets to kill Gary Williams."

"That's true," I answered. "Of course it's speculation as to whether or not they could have convicted Henry, but an eyewitness who claims he's been stabbed five times by Henry is pretty compelling evidence."

I broke the story at ten P.M. Lori Tucker and Alan Hemburger read the lead-in that started off the newscast that night:

"They're being held for the murder of a San Antonio Police officer . . ." said Lori.

"But two brothers may be responsible for much more. Our Brian Karem has been looking into the strange case of Henry David Hernandez, and has this exclusive report."

The story that followed outlined Henry's criminal past, how he tried to organize a drug dealing gang and how he terrorized some West Side residents. Leroy Chavez told us how he'd been stabbed five times and how he asked for help from the district attorney's office. Fernando Ramos told us how he couldn't find Leroy, even though I had. Finally, I quoted a police official who said he would look over Henry's criminal past to see if any of it was relevant to the current case.

It was the first Hernandez story I'd been able to

put together in nearly a month, since the confession. It was a step in the right direction, but I wasn't done yet. Of the three goals I set for myself, I'd only partially accomplished the first one: checking into the Hernandez brother's background by way of interviewing Leroy Chavez. I still had no luck getting hold of Henry's cousin again.

I also had little luck in finding out anything about Gary Williams' past, although I found an unusual ally in that department: Paul Buske. I had managed to find out that the recently divorced Williams had moved in with a dispatcher from the police department. Her name was Sue. Buske told me she had once been married to a policeman who was now dead. Because of her association with him and another officer she had earned a curious nickname downtown at the cop shop: The Black Widow.

Chapter 11

More Questions, Few Answers

The story was branching out in ways I'd never dreamed of in the beginning. I'd heard Henry was interested in joining the Mexican Mafia prison gang. Who were they? I'd heard vague references to the gang before, but knew precious little about them. Some people said Henry had been trying to form a drug dealing ring or gang on the west side of San Antonio. I'd also heard other talk of gangs and now I was beginning to wonder if San Antonio was seeing the beginnings of a street gang problem like other large American cities.

The Gary Williams' side of the story was also beginning to sprout a few shoots, but it was still very bare. Who was "The Black Widow"? Why had Gary split with his wife? Why didn't anyone on the police force seem to know anything about the man? Of course, the big questions remained: was he guilty of starting the fight with the Hernandez brothers that led to his death? Did Williams like to beat up on the citizenry?

The court hearings, of course, disrupted most of my efforts to continue pursuing the story. Ron had also instructed me to try and get ahold of Debra Ledesma and see if she would be willing to testify in court.

This turned out to be a futile effort at best. Twice I called the number she had given me and found she wasn't anywhere around. Although I'd left messages I didn't get those returned either.

The daily news didn't stop during this time, nor did my daily responsibilities. The combined pressures of court, news, sources, and helping care for an infant child were so great I began to consider a long leave of absence. Pam and our budgetary needs talked me out of that, but she became very good at telling when I was getting to the brink. Movies, especially comedies, became our personal stress outlet—that and, of course, any spare time we could muster to do something special with our son Zachary.

Just before my first hearing, Alex Ramirez came to see me and said he wanted to talk about the Hernandez story. I thought maybe he'd heard something that I could use, but instead said he was beginning to think it would be better if he came forward as a source.

"These guys are crooks, Brian," he told me. "I don't want to be in a position to protect them. I'm still a law enforcement agent and I think I should help our side."

A good feeling began to wash over me. It was fine by me if Alex wanted to come forward. I figured that would end all of my headaches because he would mention the jail guard who'd put Henry on the telephone and thereby expose the level of State involvement in helping obtain the interview with Henry Hernandez.

That had been the argument that Beth Taylor had used in the newspapers to justify her prying into my affairs, and it had been the same reason that both Goldstein and Stevens wanted my notes.

Again, I thought since everyone was so interested in what the Sheriff's department did in helping me arrange the interview with Henry, that once Alex went public, my troubles would be over.

When I mentioned this possibility to Larry and Ron, they too held out hope we'd soon be out of the courtroom and back in the news room. I only wish it had been that easy.

The day before my first court hearing I was finally able to get in touch with Debra, Henry's cousin. We had a short conversation over the telephone.

She expressed her continued concern that I was not doing my best to check into Gary Williams' past.

"I'm doing everything I can in that regard," I assured her. "Is there anything else you can tell me about Henry?"

"Not if you're going to keep picking on him."

"I'm not. I've been looking at that police officer. But it's a lot harder and no one wants to talk about him."

"He beat up Henry and nobody cares."

"I promise you, if that's the case, I care."

I left her, again, with the promise that I would not reveal her name, if she so desired. She again expressed concern that her family wouldn't like the idea of her talking with me. I said I understood and hung up the telephone.

* * *

On May 10th 1989 Larry, Ron and I made the trip to Judge Barlow's court. I felt shaky and tight.

Before we left, Sharon Adams, a former attorney, courthouse reporter, college teacher, and now one of KMOL's morning anchors came up to me. She apparently noticed my case of nerves.

"Good luck," she said.

"Thanks," I returned. Sharon and I had not been too friendly when I first got to KMOL. She'd only been there a few weeks longer than I, but for some reason we'd gotten off to a bad start.

"It's because you're an arrogant bastard," she told me.

"And you're an insufferable bitch!" I countered.

For a few months our conversations were icy, but, recently our relationship had warmed somewhat.

"I want to wish you luck," she said.

"Thanks." I was touched.

Then she smiled mischeviously. "I talked to some of my friends at the courthouse and they're going to make sure you get thrown in jail with a big guy named Bubba". She was grinning, "That could make you a big hero around here, Brian!" Now she was laughing heartily.

I began laughing too.

"Hey, if you're gone a long time in jail, you don't mind if I use your desk, do you?"

"No, go right ahead. I can give you the key, if you need to get into the locked drawer."

"No, that's okay," she advised me. "I've already got one of my own."

I walked away and noticed my apprehension had eased just a bit.

I didn't get very far when our station manager Bob Donohue met me.

"You ready?" he asked.

"I guess so. Not much choice, you know."

"Well, I want you to have this." He thrust a little white bag at me. It read, "We're behind you all the way. One hundred percent."

I was about to thank him for his kindness when I reached inside the bag and pulled out a small jar of vaseline.

"Just in case." He grinned and walked off.

Ron met me a few moments later, with no surprises, just a word of encouragement, then we walked down the street to Larry Macon's office and then all of us left for the courthouse.

We waited with added apprehension for the proceedings to begin. Since I would not reveal my sources, none of us could very well go up and ask if Alex Ramirez had talked to any of the attorneys and revealed himself.

So, we sat. I envisioned a quick mention of the revelation before the court, some discussion among the attorneys for a few minutes, then a short fifteen-minute stint on the stand for me, followed by a judge's ruling in our favor. In my mind, I had us out in time for the afternoon news.

It didn't happen that way. Alex did not go to the attorney, judge, or anyone. I spent more than an hour in the witness stand grilled in exhaustive cross examination by the city's best prosecution and defense attorneys. It was not fun.

The Hernandez brothers sat at a table directly across from me. Henry was small and quiet, his brother taller and equally passive. They both wore the bright orange jail coveralls issued to jail inmates, and spent the time staring at the proceedings as if it were a TV program or a circus of freaks.

Though they sat stoically through most of the proceedings, I saw both Julian and Henry grin at least once.

I didn't feel very amused, and was angry that the whole thing had gone this far. Someone, I was sure, should have stopped this nonsense by now.

But no one did.

Judge James Barlow's acid comments on the long delay expressed my own frustration.

"All right. Now, let's see, I will be glad when they indict this case and it gets assigned to some judge and he can handle it and I don't have to worry about this any more. This is another saga in Julian Hernandez and his brother . . ."

Judge Barlow, while serving as the judge who magistrated the Hernandez brothers into jail actually had no case pending before him. Ultimately the Texas Criminal Court of Appeals would rule that Barlow had no right to throw me in jail. He had no reason to hold a hearing. After the judge's brief introduction I was sworn in and Larry Macon began to ask me questions. His direct examination lasted less than two minutes:

"Are you the reporter that was involved in the telephone conversation relating to the Hernandez matter?"

"Yes, sir; I was."

"Has KMOL turned over all the tapes that exist with respect to that telephone conversation?"

"I believe we handed them over to the judge—all that exists after editing, yes."

"And was there any deletion or editing done after any subpoenas were served on Channel Four?"

"No sir.

"In addition, in addition to the tapes, did you—do you—have any notes that relate to this matter?"

"Yes, sir; I do."

"What are on those notes?"

"Well, confidential sources, their names and phone numbers."

"There are no transcripts of what Mr. Hernandez or someone claiming to be Mr. Hernandez said on TV, are there?"

"No."

"Do you believe that those tapes should not be turned over?"

"I believe the tapes should not be turned over and I believe my notes should not be turned over."

"Tell the court why you believe your notes should not be turned over?"

"I believe the notes should not be turned over because I believe I have a privilege to protect those people that I promised I would protect—my sources."

Larry, about done now, capped off his questioning: "And did you promise the sources that are listed on those notes that you would not turn those over?"

"Yes, I did."

I took a breath after Larry's short round of questions. They'd been softballs. I sat up straight and waited for what would happen next.

Mark Stevens, who has handled some very difficult Capital Murder cases as well as some work for the American Civil Liberty's Union, led off.

His first questions centered around how my telephone number got to Henry Hernandez. I thought this was natural since he still probably labored under a misconception that I'd been inside the jail and had a face-to-face meeting with Henry. "I told them there's no way we would allow a reporter inside the jail to talk to a suspect without a judge's approval," Alex told me. Apparently, though, Alex did not reveal his role in the interview. The judge, my attorney, and Mark hashed that all out for a while. Then Gerald Goldstein jumped in citing all kinds of cases that he said demonstrated I had no right to protect my sources in this case.

The judge grumbled, rubbed his face, then bellowed out in that distinctly gruff voice, "Why do I get the feeling we are trying this case before we get to it?"

Larry, quick to notice anything remotely favorable to his case, piped in with, "You are a hundred percent right."

Didnt' matter, and we quickly lost the edge. Prosecutor Beth Taylor, who's also fairly quick on her feet, decided to toss her gasoline on the fire:

"For me to fully conduct the investigation, which one must do before one indicts a case, I need to know this information. I need to know if this man, Brian Karem, was acting as an agent of the State."

Her argument was that someone, perhaps a police officer, who couldn't get to Henry Hernandez might have coerced me into trying to get the interview with him. I grinned; the chances of that were only slightly better than me discovering the origin of the universe.

Things only got sillier. Gerald Goldstein (whose clientele includes Dr. Hunter S. Thompson, and who also does work for the ACLU) decided he would take the prosecutor's role.

"The grand jury, I have heard, is entitled to every man's evidence. We, on the other hand, need to know that in order to prepare an adequate defense," Goldstein opened.

Judge Barlow, a former prosecutor, looked slightly aghast.

"Are you sure which side you are on?" A small smile spread quietly across the judge's face.

"I didn't support it, I just said I have heard it a lot," Goldstein said as he displayed his well known impish grin.

Judge Barlow shook his head and rubbed his massive hands across his face. "First I have ever heard you argue *that*."

Done with his asides, Goldstein got back to business. "Well, it kind of stuck a little bit. Having said it, I will stick by it."

For a while I thought the judge might just end it right there. Things had gotten so ridiculous. Barlow said he thought I was entitled to the communications I had with my sources, but that opinion evaporated as soon as everyone tried to pin me down on what was actually in my notes—although I had already said it was nothing more than names and telephone numbers.

Goldstein and Stevens both began to argue that there was no other way to find out who my sources were—other than my testimony. This was going too far. I did not have a telephone conversation with myself. I had talked to Henry. If I knew who all three sources were, Henry had to know even better than me. He had the note passed to him. He was placed at the telephone by a jailer. He called his cousin. All I did was answer a telephone call from him. I brought this up in court when I found a moment to squeeze in a word:

"Excuse me," I broke in. "May I ask a question at this point?"

It is extremely rare for a witness to ask a question from the stand, but by now Barlow was past shock and surprise. He just nodded his head and said "Uh-huh."

I pointed at Goldstein and mustering all the righteous indignation I could, queried him. "You say we can't get it from any other source. The information I got was from your client. You have no greater access to your client than I do?"

Goldstein's smile flickered before he answered. I had no idea why, although afterwards he told me he enjoyed watching a witness for once get in as many questions as the attorneys. With a full grin planted firmly on his face, he said simply, "It is not my client." Mark Stevens, who was in no mood to answer questions from witnesses, spoke up. "It is my client."

I turned to Mark. "You have no greater access to your client than I do?"

"You don't get to ask the questions."

Mark looked angry, although Gerald quickly told me he wasn't. I wasn't angry either, but I thought my questions pointed out the absurdity of grilling me when they could ask their clients just as easily.

But, I could convince no one of this position. Although I thought getting client-attorney information would be easier than turning me upside down and shaking me to see what fell loose. No one seemed to have seriously considered questioning anyone *but* me and KMOL's news department about our stories.

I looked closely at Mark Stevens who was blowing a tremendous amount of smoke trying to obtain something his own client already had. The motive, as it turns out, is easy enough to understand. Everyone knows the longer you can postpone a criminal trial, the better it is for the defense. Documents disappear, witnesses forget important details, and some witnesses may no longer be around by the time you get to trial—if you postpone the day of reckoning long enough.

The longer Mark kept Henry from going to trial, the better his chances were of keeping his client from a conviction—and possible lethal injection. I had conveniently provided Mark with a means of pursuing his ends. He was bright enough to sink his briefcase into it.

Meanwhile, Beth Taylor jumped back in and began arguing she couldn't indict the Hernandez brothers without my testimony and my notes—so crucial was my interview with Henry to their case. This had a false ring to it also. I had seen witness statements from more than half a dozen people, including the security guard, who had actually seen part of the crime—something I hadn't done. So again, I tried to ask a question. I raised my hand and looked at Barlow:

"Excuse me. May I?"

Barlow swung around and looked at me. Then he turned and looked at the attorneys who were more than a little startled that a witness had the audacity to ask still another question. Barlow was quick with a "Yes."

Goldstein gave me another amiable grin. "Sure," he said. I was glad I could be of amusement to him. But, I leveled my question at Beth Taylor.

"It is my understanding, from the information I received from the police department, which you should well have, and I am sure you already do, there were complainants and witnesses at the scene. Why would this information be needed by you?"

"You don't tell me how to run my case."

Her answer had no trace of humor in it. Judge Barlow and Goldstein were both openly grinning now. I looked over and saw even the Hernandez brothers were enjoying this sideshow act. In fact, although even Mark Stevens was now grinning at the loud retort that had erupted from the district attorney. Beth, however, was having no part of it. Some may have even called Beth's high pitched cacophony rude. I decided I wouldn't be bullied.

"Well, I am asking."

"You don't ask what my information is. That is not your job."

I respect Beth as one of the finest prosecutors in San Antonio. But asking her what information she has is what my job's all about.

The lawyers in their impeccable suits argued the points of law for a few more minutes and then Barlow, worn down by the sheer numbing effect of having four lawyers plus one witness scream questions for close to an hour, decided to give in to the prosecution and defense's demands. He gave me until Friday to turn in my notes or face going to jail.

As Larry and I filed out of the courtroom with Ron, I took stock of the proceedings. We'd lost round one, sure enough, but Barlow seemed about to rule in our favor on a couple of occasions. Beth and Mark had been surly, but Goldstein had greeted me with a pat on the back as I left. Maybe we'd win this thing.

"You think maybe Barlow will listen to us on Friday?" I asked Larry.

He extinguished my hopes with an acrid bit of reality. "He ruled today. He's not going to change his mind by Friday."

That didn't sound good. Ron had nothing to add that would bolster my spirits. He said he'd been against this from the very start. "You can turn over the notes without shame," he said. "You did your best to fight it today."

Maybe his words were meant to cheer me up. They didn't.

That night Pam and I talked about my position. To me it was a sacrosanct rule: a reporter never parts with his notes. A reporter never divulges a source. Court rulings may come or go in support of that ideal, but with me the ideal could never change.

"What if you have nothing in your notes?" Pam asked me.

"That's the whole point. I don't. I don't even think

my sources can help the case very much. Everything's already on the record that Henry said and that's what matters."

"I understand," Pam was unequivocal in her support. We'd gone through a lot together and as a former reporter she agreed with how I felt.

Friday came. I still refused to hand my notes over to Barlow. Suddenly the game became very serious. He decided to toss me into jail.

After his ruling, he afforded me the opportunity to visit with my attorney. Larry looked as nervous and upset as I felt. He took my wedding ring, watch, belt, tie, and wallet since those things would be confiscated once I got inside the jail.

"Don't worry," he told me. He had the omnipresent grin.

"Thanks Larry." I said stiffly, and turned to the bailiff who would cuff me. We knew each other.

"Sorry, Brian." He put on the cuffs.

Ron looked down and then said slowly, "We'll try and get you out today." I left the courtroom in handcuffs and walked down the same hall that Julian and Henry Hernandez had less than two months previously. Some of the same reporters gathered to watch me just as they had gathered to witness the Hernandez walk.

I grinned as I often do when I'm nervous. Juli Branson, a *San Antonio Light* reporter managed to get my attention.

"Why are you doing this, Brian?"

"It's a little thing called the First Amendment and I feel very strongly about it," I said quietly. Then I slowly walked down the hall to the prisoners' elevator. I'd just travelled from one end of the camera to the other. It was a long and painful trip.

Chapter 12

Jail House Blues

I rode to jail in a Bexar County detention van with a wino I'm sure had not seen a shower, comb, or clean clothes for several days. I was bemoaning my plight until I saw this man. It put things into perspective. Then the man spoke to me.

"Whatcha do? Forget to make the alimony payment?"

On the last syllable he gave a drunken belch and spewed some foul smelling brown liquid on the floor. I could no longer feel sorry for him.

The ride ended moments later.

Larry Macon and Ron Harig had alerted the sheriff that I would be coming to jail, and I was greeted by the jail administrator, the Chief Deputy, the sheriff, and the Director of Human Services upon my arrival.

Considering I was entering jail as a prisoner instead of a reporter, it was quite a greeting and helped calm my nerves, which were shot.

Following the friendly greetings by the jail hierarchy, I went through the unavoidable paperwork of prints, mug shots, and property inventory. Then, I went upstairs to the office of Mike Martin, one of the assistant jail administrators. There I got to rest, use the telephone, and take a nap. It made me feel better that I was staying inside someone's office. Still I knew this was very temporary. I was incarcerated. If Larry couldn't get an appeal and bond posted, then I was going to be in deep trouble. I didn't look forward to spending a weekend inside the Bexar County Jail, wearing orange jail togs and sleeping on a metal cot.

I called Zachary's day care to let them know I might be a little late in picking up my son. Pam was, unfortunately, out of town on business and my primary concern was getting Zachary home and taken care of. I had no relatives living in town at the time, Pam and I had only a few close personal friends, none of whom could help me out now; so I was worried.

The day care director offered to have someone stay with Zachary if I needed that convenience, and finally I was able to rest a little easier.

A short time later Mike Martin came up to see me. He asked if I wanted anything to eat or drink, and when I answered, yes, he produced a lovely soybean burger and a cup of coffee from the Bexar County jail's cafeteria. I didn't complain. I was getting royal service for a jail and even if the burger was my only meal of the day, who was I to gripe?

"Get you anything else, Rocky?" Mike grinned at me.

"Nah, warden," I said. "This cup of java and boiga' ought to do."

While I sweated out incarceration inside the jail, Larry and Ron had the infinitely more arduous task of facing our cohorts in the press.

Most reporters were concerned with my well being. Juli Branson, the *San Antonio Light* reporter, noted that prior to the hearing I had joked about what I thought was a remote possibility of going to jail.

"When they started taking away his personal effects, that's when the chill came," Macon said. "It's no game."

Ron, despite any private arguments earlier, now showed his support.

"We tried to be cooperative in every way because of the nature of the case," Ron told the assembled throng of reporters inside the jail lobby. "But we had to draw the line."

"We think the right to confidential sources is very important," Macon told the press. "Unless the news media stands up and protects their confidential sources, then those sources will dry up; and freedom of the press is going to mean very little.

"It shouldn't be a reporter's job to do investigations for the prosecution."

Kevin Johnson, a *San Antonio Light* reporter and president of the Society of Professional Journalists, San Antonio Chapter, added, "By providing videotapes and other recordings, the television station has been more than cooperative with the court. It is time for the State to get on with its own investigation of the crime. A reporter cannot be expected to do the job of the State. The court's demands are totally unreasonable."

"Ridiculous!" is how the Society's Houston director, Ira Perry, labeled Barlow's decision. "If they have a leak within the jail, it's their responsibility to find it without trampling all over the First Amendment," Perry said. "No one would ever talk to a reporter if they knew a reporter's notes were immediately available under court order."

The lines were now drawn and the war began in earnest. What started as a spirited debate that I thought would end with little fuss, had turned deadly serious.

Never again would the attorneys or judge be as amicable as in the first court hearing, and never would KMOL have even the sliver of hope that was held out for us in that hearing.

The ripple effects were enormous, first in the state of Texas and later outside of it. This first court decision had repercussions that affected *Corpus Christi* reporter Libby Averyt who would spend a night in jail, and two newspaper reporters from Houston who would also face jail time for doing essentially the same thing I did.

After the short news conference, Macon filed a motion to have me released from jail pending an appeal of Barlow's decision.

Barlow granted the emergency motion that allowed me to be freed after booking procedures, but only after Macon posted a $2,000 cash bond.

"The good news is I got you out," Larry told me as he gave me back my wedding ring, wallet, and neck tie. "The bad news is we'll have to go through this all over again next week."

"Do we have any better chance next week?" I so wanted to hope.

"Hard to say. But it's before Barlow and he's already ruled against you once. I don't expect it'll be much better next week."

"That doesn't sound very encouraging." I offered.

"It isn't." Larry comiserated.

"I told you what it was going to be like," Ron ventured. "It's not going to get any better."

Meanwhile Beth Taylor kept loudly insisting that I give up my notes and sources.

"I cannot get an indictment without knowing

who these sources are," she told me and everyone else.

She also informed reporters that she needed to know who set up the interview to see if I really *had* interviewed Henry Hernandez—an issue that had already been put to rest in court, but one she happily paraded in front of those who hadn't sat in on every minute of court testimony.

Ironically, my jailing occurred only a few hours after a State Senate panel in Austin approved a "shield law" for journalists that would exempt us from contempt proceedings when we tried to protect our sources.

State Senator Frank Tejeda said news reports several weeks ago about the controversy over my notes had led him to go forward with the bill.

"It's my feeling that journalists should not be used as investigators or pawns by litigants in either a civil or criminal trial," he said.

The measure died.

But we at KMOL had little time to worry about such things. We directed our efforts toward trying to get as many attorneys on our side as possible.

Larry was as cooperative as ever in this regard and encouraged other local media to get involved. We got friends from the court briefs filed from the local newspapers, and from newspaper and television stations across the state.

I struggled to rally other media support. I wrote letters to the Society of Professional Journalists, the Reporters Committee for Freedom of the Press, Investigative Reporters and Editors, and every other organization remotely concerned with reporters' rights.

Steve Weinberg, then executive director of I.R.E. was the first to get back with me. I.R.E. is a small organization of about three thousand journalists, who in the immortal words of NBC's Jim Polk, are the "dedicated last bastion between real journalism and the bean counters."

Weinberg wrote a letter to Judge Barlow which noted that KMOL ". . . already turned over unaired tape. That is farther than most journalists would go . . ."

I gave the letter to Larry the following Friday, May 19th as we walked over to Barlow's courtroom. It was my second trip there and Larry and Ron's third.

The second appearance went much differently than the first. Before Barlow even started, he called the principles into his chambers for a closed door meeting.

Mark Cannan, a local media attorney who'd filed a brief in Barlow's court in our behalf, protested this closed door session most vigorously.

"Let him yell!" Barlow said defiantly.

Then he closed the door.

"Now before we begin," Barlow counseled us, "we have a problem with this so I want to be sure that everybody understands, and everybody is on the same frequency." As it turned out, the problem Barlow was referring to was Alex Ramirez. Alex had talked to Barlow the day before in the judge's chambers.

Barlow recapped their conversation. "He says, 'I am the source, the guy that gave him the note,' And I said, well, wait a minute. I don't want to be talking to you at all. I am the judge. I am going to advise counsel what you are telling me, and I am going to ask you to be there in the morning, whatever. And that is the gist of it."

I breathed a heavy sigh of relief. This was it. Ramirez had come forward. I no longer had to protect him. The State and the defense would now learn the total amount of involvement the sheriff's department had in helping me interview Henry Hernandez without my help. They could put Alex on the stand and question everyone else involved.

I looked around. I didn't see any startled faces on the assembled attorneys, but then again they're good at playing poker. "I don't know whether you knew that, or whether that makes any difference," Barlow added. "Or whether that changes anything or anything else."

Yes, of course it did, I wanted to shout!

"But, apparently, he did tell me." Barlow said, "I never told him to call anyone; in fact, I told him not to." The judge now stared at us all. ". . . And I never meant to get myself in a position where I am talking to a witness. But under the circumstances, that is not an unusual thing, for me to talk to bailiffs in the courtroom. I mean it is just one of those deals.

"I wanted you to know where we were. I don't know whether it makes any difference to anybody or anything else. If you are ready to have the hearing . . ."

The judge's voice trailed off. I was elated. It was all out in the open. I wanted to say, I kept my word and now the attorneys know how the State helped set up the interview. Game's over. Let's all go home.

Unfortunately no one else wanted to stop playing. "I believe we need to go ahead with the hearing," Larry Macon finally said.

"I appreciate you telling us," Larry added as a final note.

We all filed out of the chambers more glum than a few minutes before. I was spending more time in court than in the news room. We took our places in open court.

As Barlow made his introductions to begin the day's proceedings, I tried to talk to Larry. "What the hell is going on *now?*" I asked.

"Just wait," he answered quickly.

Then, before we could get started, a second interruption occurred. This time Mark Cannan jumped up, and announcing that he was appearing on behalf of five different media organizations, including the Society of Profession Journalists and Harte Hanks Communications, and protested the closed door session which had just ended.

"Who are you?" asked Barlow.

"I am their lawyer," came Cannan's obvious reply.

"I am sorry I kicked you out of my back room, then."

"That is the point I would like to make at this time."

The judge chuckled. "I thought you were some overwrought reporter."

"Underpaid, probably," Cannan shot back.

Cannan was able to obtain a copy of the transcript from the closed door proceedings, which would let everyone in town know that Alex Ramirez was the man who'd set up my interview with Henry Hernandez.

To me, it boiled down to the fact that everything everyone wanted to know, or claimed to want to know, was out in the open. And it didn't matter. Five minutes later the court proceedings were adjourned. I hadn't spoken a word and I was sent to jail for the second time in a week.

The second time I went to the Bexar County slammer I didn't get the same privileged treatment as the first time. Shortly after my arrival, I was subjected to the intimate touch and feel session known as a patdown.

It's a slap in the face that robs you of your dignity and serves to remind you that once inside jail, your life is not your own.

"Turn around. Hands against the wall. Spread your legs apart." The woman telling me this was about five feet tall. She was built like a fireplug and had her hair in a bun. On her hands she wore a pair of thin, clear, disposable rubber gloves.

"Now!"

I looked hard at her. "No need to be rude." I said as sweetly as I could. After all, this was my second time through this process. Before I knew it, and without any pain, she spun me around. I quickly "assumed the position."

She proceeded to search my pockets, then felt around my neck and down my legs. She looked in my sleeves and had me take off my shoes. Then she checked the shoes. When she reached in the region of my groin, I jumped.

"You must enjoy your work," I said.

"Stay still," she monotoned. Then after a pause, "And yes, I do. Now turn around." She never cracked a grin.

She handed me my shoes and ushered me to a desk. No doubt the woman was a pro, I thought. She worked with precision, cold and calm. I wondered how many people she's searched and then I thought about how dangerous her job could be. A thin veneer of disassociation from some harsh realities might not be such a bad thing.

Sitting down in a metal chair bolted to the concrete floor I waited for someone to process my paper work. A couple of deputies I knew came over and exchanged greetings.

I was told by Sergeant Carlos Santiago, the man who runs the booking floor, "The Sheriff said he'd never let a reporter in his jail. I guess you proved him a liar." He laughed. I chuckled lightly.

The rest of the day wasn't that amusing. Finally, in the late afternoon, I was sprung.

Chapter 13

Dead in the Water

On hot spring and summer days in San Antonio, of which there are usually more than most residents in that fair city care to deal with, reporters have been known to do some strange things.

For example, Bryan Glazer. Before the former, KENS reporter was arrested and charged with changing the price tags on a couple of house plants at a local grocery store, he made a name for himself in San Antonio with pair of eggs.

He tried to fry them on the asphalt of a parking lot during a live-shot in the middle of a newscast. Granted it was hot outside, and granted many people have often said it's hot enough in San Antonio to fry an egg on the sidewalk, but donating two minutes of valuable news time so the home viewers could watch runny eggs fail to congeal on some unknown city parking lot was not a high-point in local television news.

Nor was the live-shot a local television reporter did at a nudist colony during ratings month.

Local viewers in that case were treated to a wide assortment of videotape clips of bulbous rear ends walking into a hot tub, naked people crossing their legs, the odd long shot of women's breasts and one side view tight-shot of a naked man's pubic hairs softly easing themselves into the hot tub between the man's pasty white thighs.

In both stories, credibility suffered, other reporters laughed, and some members of the viewing public displayed attitudes ranging from criticism to skepticism. Of course, both stories were watched by a huge viewing audience. In television, a big ratings boost will usually justify a questionable venture into the lurid, laughable, and/or unethical.

Many who've spent more than few years in television news now believe it is dying, as stations sacrifice long term credibility and the serious business of reporting news for the novel, off-beat, or the erotic story that has little news value but grabs ratings points.

Local newspapers are not immune to this syndrome. I've worked for more than a few who've run certain stories, because they appeal to big advertisers. More than a few reporters from small to large newspapers can tell similar horror stories. Don't even ask those reporters what they think of "Wingo" and other marketing tools designed to boost circulation.

This ugly side to the press has many professionals fearful of the future of journalism in general. Some managers, professors, and even television station owners and newspaper owners see dwindling incomes and wonder what they're doing wrong. It says something that many never figure out what the dissatisfied viewers and readers already know.

Not long after Gary Williams' death, I got to witness firsthand the ugly side of the press in San Antonio.

On Monday, May 22nd 1989, I got into work early. I expected to confer with Ron and our attorney about what steps we should take next. After all, the previous Friday I had gone to jail.

It was beginning to look like a habit. The Friday before that, on May 12th, I had also gone to jail. Both times I didn't know if or when I would get out. Both times I was told I would probably have to spend the weekend in jail at the very least. But, both times Larry Macon got me out late that afternoon.

Before I could even reach my desk, Ron handed me a copy of the Friday afternoon *San Antonio Light*.

Suddenly I got my introduction into "being the story" instead of just covering the story. The papers headline read "Rights of free media, fair trial will clash in court again."

The article, penned by two of the paper's veteran reporters, talked about the interview I obtained with Henry Hernandez and the court battle which had just begun because of it.

> *"In the KMOL case, Karem aired March 28 a purported telephone interview with Henry David Hernandez . . .*
>
> *Karem has claimed he received a telephone call from a person identifying himself as Henry David Hernandez after the brothers already had been taken into custody by police.*
>
> *KMOL presented the story as if it was a jailhouse interview.*
>
> *. . . But courthouse sources said an unaired segment of the tape indicates the interview was made before the arrest of Hernandez.*
>
> *Answering that question was the aim of the order that Karem turn over his notes and unedited tape. When the interview was conducted will be the key factor in deciding whether the purported confession is admissible in the trial of Hernandez.*

> *The Karem interview abruptly ends with the voice of the person being interviewed saying he had to get off the telephone because police were coming to arrest him.*
>
> *If that is true, then it would appear the interview did not take place from the jail. And if it did not, did KMOL make assumptions it should not have made in its presentation of the news report?"*

I stopped reading and turned to Ron.
"What the hell is this?" I asked.
"Have you finished yet?"
"No."
"Finish it."
I glanced back down at the paper.

> *". . . Did KMOL act responsibly in airing the purported interview and involving itself in a criminal proceeding?*
>
> *Judge Barlow has said he thinks the dispute between his court and KMOL is the most difficult he has encountered, and eventually will have to be settled in the appellate courts.*
>
> *. . . The court is attempting to discover, among other things, who set up the interview for Karem from the jail, if indeed the telephone call was placed from there. The state had demanded Karem's notes to establish exactly when the interview took place. Prosecutors say they suspect the tape was made prior to Hernandez's arrest. If it was, the confession would be admissible in a criminal prosecution.*
>
> *Gerald Goldstein, the defense attorney representing Julian Hernandez, wants Karem's notes because he believes they may help exonerate his client.*

Mark Stevens, who represents Henry Hernandez, needs to know if his client was interviewed while in jail because, if he was, the taped confession would not be admissible.

"I've got a really big problem here," Barlow said in an interview prior to this morning's ruling. "This is a classic clash between the First Amendment calling for a free press and the Sixth Amendment that guarantees a defendant's right to a fair trial. But this is a case not nearly as simple as others that have come up before."

I tossed the paper down and looked at Ron.

"What a crock of shit," I said through clenched teeth.

"Is any of it true?" He asked as calmly as he says everything.

I was indignant "What? You were here! Which part should I tell you about? No, we didn't interview Henry before his arrest! No, he never said he was getting arrested. No, we didn't make any false assumptions about the interview. And, no, we didn't act irresponsibly!"

He took a deep breath. "Brian, I told you this was going to happen. We're probably going to take harder hits than this because of the story. Are you still up to it?"

I choked down what was beginning to be my daily dose of panic.

"What do you mean? Do you want me to turn over my notes? Aren't we going to fight this any more?

"That decision hasn't been made yet. But I've told you all along I don't think this is a case we can go to the wall for."

My mind raced. It had been almost six weeks since we'd had this kind of conversation. I thought everything was settled. I'd already gone to jail twice. How could things change now?

"Well, I do," was all I could say.

"I know." Ron countered. "But how many times do you think you can handle going to jail? This is an emotional roller coaster you know, and not only for you."

He was absolutely right. The strain was showing on just about everyone in the newsroom. Then, of course, there was the strain on my wife.

We all felt pressured and anxious, perhaps I, whose decision had caused the problem, more than anyone else.

I hadn't much time to dwell on his words. A short while later, both Beth Taylor and Mark Stevens announced they still needed to have my notes to find out if any of my sources were "an agent of the State."

Taylor said revealing my sources could be used to determine if the man I interviewed really was Henry Hernandez, and that if my source were revealed it might determine whether or not the confession could be admissible in court.

No one was listening to Alex Ramirez and Macon was upset.

"The State hasn't shown how the names of these people (sources) would help them get an indictment," Macon told local reporters. "It's incredible to me the State still hasn't been able to get an indictment and now is looking for a reporter to do their work for them."

The following week the local columnists got involved in the story. The first was Rick Casey, a front page columnist for the *San Antonio Light*.

"For most of us in print journalism, this is a difficult, if fascinating, situation. On the one hand, we don't like alleged cop killers. On the other, we like TV reporters even less."

"It's comforting to know I rate somewhere below alleged cop killers," I told Larry. "I wonder if that's above or below lawyers and newspaper columnists on the food chain?"

Larry laughed and told me to hang in there. He was not appealing my case before the State's Criminal Court of Appeals, the highest court available to us in the state.

"What happens if we lose *there?*" I asked. You see, I was beginning to think seriously.

"We have to go the federal route and hope someone will hear the case on our constitutional grounds. But don't worry about that right now. Let's win this thing at the state level and go home," Larry said.

"I'm all for that!" I said emphatically, and left him alone to get back to the grindstone.

Meanwhile, everyone was adding their opinion to the growing controversy.

Casey ended up writing two columns about the mess, and while slamming television reporters in general, he did defend the principle of keeping a promise of confidentiality.

I got a couple of calls from local radio talk show hosts around the country. They asked me to take part in discussions about the First Amendment.

Macon even jumped on the band wagon and wrote a column that appeared in the *San Antonio Light* the second week of June.

"The tradition of freedom of the press is strong: Newspaper editor Ben Franklin was called on the carpet by a congressional committee for refusing to reveal his sources. Karem is in good company," he wrote.

Larry also noted that there was no compelling

need for me to disclose my sources, and despite the drama of an alleged cop killer and a taped confession, "Karem's notes are not the only way to find out who his "inside track" was. Karem should be cut from the cast of characters and the trial should play itself out."

Finally, Larry talked a little about the history of the First Amendment and said as late as the 1960s and 70s there was a strong movement toward First Amendment protection.

"Justices William O. Douglas and Hugo Black of the Supreme Court said that the First Amendment was absolute and untouchable. In came Richard Nixon, and later Ronald Reagan appointees, and more conservative opinions drowned out the liberal voices. Suddenly, there were no absolutes in the Constitution. Rights like freedom of the press were weighted against societal needs."

That was the last word on the case until the end of June. Then the Court of Criminal Appeals notified us they would hear our case after they came back from their summer recess—probably in September.

Finally, we would have a break. For the next three months, at least, I would be able to concentrate on work. The prospect of jail once again dimmed as the grind of every day life took over.

I tried to pick up the trail on the Hernandez and Williams' ends of the story. But leads were growing cold and stale. Between the posturing, arguing, and postponements of the court, KMOL was left dead in the water. Follow-ups to our original story were almost impossible. People were increasingly difficult to find. After several months, memories were already beginning to fade. Paperwork was filed away and forgotten. And, in some cases, the notoriety of the case was scaring off some who might talk.

But, the most difficult problem in finding out the truth in the Gary Williams' story was that no one wanted to talk. Gary Williams' girlfriend didn't want to talk, nor did his family. For a while it looked like there would be no more stories about the Hernandez brothers or Williams.

Then one morning I received a yellow folder. I opened it and looked carefully at a copy of a typewritten letter. It was addressed to Chief Bill Gibson and dated January 18th, 1987. This made me curious, because I wasn't sure Gibson was chief at the time. If this was a phony letter, I could quickly tell by finding out if Gibson was police chief in January of 1987. A telephone call later I found out that Gibson had been appointed acting chief in November of 1986 and took over the position permanently in April of 1987. So, the letter passed my first test.

A further quick check showed the letter had been mailed to Mayor Henry Cisneros, Councilman Jim Hasslocher, City Manager Lou Fox and to the *Express-News* Columnist, Paul Thompson. I called all of them to see if they'd indeed received it. Everyone at the city referred me to the police department's internal affairs office where I got the customary, "No Comment."

I really didn't expect a call back from Paul Thompson, who until his death was the heaviest hitter among local columnists, but he surprised me.

Paul promised faithfully to see if he still had a copy or had ever run across a copy of the communication.

The police department supplied me with the exact dates that Gibson took over the department's reins and since it turned out that he began his stint in office before the letter was alleged to be written, I decided to do a serious follow-up on the letter writer.

It turned out to be written by Ken Suhler, a man who was upset that his two sons in the northeast Fox Run subdivision had been given tickets and handcuffed by Gary Williams.

"Williams' attitude was surly, petulant, and belligerent," Ken Suhler wrote. The man said Williams harassed his two sons while making a routine traffic stop and his attitude was similar to Stephen Smith's well documented vigilante antics.

Suhler contacted Williams' superiors who said Williams was one of the departments' best officers and had no previous complaints against him. Then, in what appeared to be an eerie bit of prophecy, Suhler concluded that Williams was ". . . a bad apple," and it was only "a matter of time" before he got into something more serious.

I put down the letter.

Things were beginning to smell really badly as far as Williams was concerned, and I knew I had to be careful. Police officers do not routinely get involved in fist fights, and it's been my experience that they are usually on the receiving end of blows much more than on the giving end. Every cop reporter knows it's often a tough call for cops to determine when to use force and how much force to use. They have their academy training that says one thing; the reality of the streets that often says something else; and the politics of the city that will judge them another way entirely.

Cops live in morbid fear of the "Monday morning quarterbacking" that goes on every time they must use force. It teaches the best of them to be judicious and careful. And, the rules of the game dictate that all force must stop once the handcuffs go on. Even if the prisoner kicks, bites, shoves, or manages to continue the fight in another way, the cop must never use force on a cuffed prisoner.

To do so is an immediate suspension and a violation of the prisoner's civil rights. Cursing, threatening, or any other type of verbal abuse can lead to the same thing.

Still, even when brutality does occur, it's many times tough to prove to the point an officer gets suspended. It's harder still to put a story in the newspaper or on television about the brutality *unless* the officer has been suspended or prosecuted. The chance for a libel suit is overwhelming. Often witnesses and the accused officer have little desire to go to the press. Sometimes the witnesses are lying. Sometimes they're legitimately afraid. Sometimes their fear is ungrounded. Sometimes it's not.

The officers, obviously don't wish to be second guessed. Either they've done their job as instructed, or they haven't. Since it's a judgment call they'd rather have their brother officers judge them than the media. If they're right, they hope to be vindicated, if they're wrong they're hoping for protection from their own.

Some cities have instituted a citizens' review board so the average voter can take a part in the punishment of these officers, but San Antonio is not one of them. Despite the Tucker-Smith scandal, San Antonio has not shown any inclination to adopt such measures. Chief Bill Gibson is dead set against it. He says the average citizen will be more lenient with bad cops than other cops will. The upshot is that for a variety of reasons reporting on police brutality is one of the most difficult tasks facing any police beat reporter.

I hoped I was taking every precaution necessary in the Gary Williams' case because Debra Ledesman's words that night on the telephone with Henry Hernandez seemed to haunt me.

Could Gary have picked the fight? Was he one of

the officers often heard about, but seldom met by the press, who liked to "tune up" the citizenry for some twisted and self-serving reason? I'd never met the man, and I had no desire to unfairly accuse him, especially since he was dead. Still, things didn't seem right.

The next lead came from Thompson, who called me back and said he'd done some preliminary checking into the case, but had never looked at it any closer. However, he did know that according to a newspaper account back in 1987, Gary Williams had an accident, turning over his police cruiser enroute to joining a chase. Did that help? he asked.

I thanked him and said I had no idea.

In fact, I had no idea where any of this was going. I was wrapped up in court battles, trying to stay out of jail. I was working my daily beat and covering whatever craziness the denizens of San Antonio had in mind on any given day, and all the while I was striving to pick up the pieces to a cold story.

Once again I picked up the yellow folder with Suhler's letter, thoroughly reread it, and then decided to go over the other paperwork I'd accumulated. There were several witness statements, newspaper accounts, and even the autopsy report to go through.

I took one day off, stayed at home and called everyone I could think of about the case. Among those people was Greg Trimble. He'd been a mystery from the beginning and I wondered if he might shed some light on what was going on. But at this point he'd had little time to devote to the case. He promised me if he found out anything, he'd let me know.

Not promising. Nothing from anyone else seemed to help either. Stevens wouldn't talk to me. Although Goldstein would, he didn't have much to say. He did laugh, God bless him, when I suggested I should talk to his client.

Beth Taylor wouldn't even return my telephone calls and the police had no desire to talk to me about anything involving a homicide, much less Gary Williams.

The witnesses weren't willing to talk either. In fact a few had reported that the police had warned them not to talk to the press. That's not surprising, though, homicide detectives do that in just about every case.

"You're trying too hard," Pam advised me.

I couldn't argue with her, but her words didn't help my frustration. The notes sat in my study next to my computer as they had since the subpoena. Every once in a while I took them out and stared. One page with telephone numbers, names, and bad doodles was what everyone wanted. Why not give it to them and have the last laugh?

Pam told me to relax; she felt I was taking things too seriously. Probably I was.

I tried to take her advice, but I couldn't forget the case. A few nights later I found myself sitting at my desk, rubbing my head, and pondering what course to try next. I'd gone over every witness statement, every lead, every source. Everything was falling through. Picking up the Williams' autopsy report, more out of desperation than anything else, I began pondering it once again. I scrutinized every word. I'd read these findings, more times than I could remember. There was mention of poorly digested onions found in Gary's stomach along with about 400 cc's of "dark brown hemorrhagic fluid." Not very appetizing.

Nor were the descriptions of the bruises, the bite marks, and the gunshot wound very pleasing to read about.

Then, once again I went over the toxicology report. There was no alcohol noted nor any acids. The alkaline screen showed the presence of lidocaine, probably from the surgery and efforts to save his life, I thought. Nothing else was noteworthy. However, I did notice that there was no mention of the amounts of lidocaine in Gary's blood stream. Usually a toxicology report mentions some amount. Probably nothing, but I decided to check with the medical examiner the next day.

"The toxicology report isn't back yet," Dr. Vincent DiMaio, the medical examiner shrugged.

"Well, what is in the autopsy report?" I asked.

"That's just very preliminary stuff. It takes a while to get the full toxicology results back."

Blood samples are always taken in circumstances similar to Gary Williams' death. The extensive blood work often takes several weeks to complete, but DiMaio told me it would be available in a few days.

There still was a big question. Hernandez had said Williams had a strange attitude. There had been the ugly spectre raised about the possibility of drug use. I, and I assumed everyone else, had put those questions to rest because of the autopsy report.

Now, the answer had changed. Indeed there seemed to be no answer at all. Only questions.

"Do you really think there's anything to this, or is it just wishful thinking?" Ron asked when I informed him what I'd found out.

"I don't know. I'll keep checking and see what I get."

"Okay, but we don't do any stories until we find out what's in that autopsy report."

"Agreed," I said thoughtfully.

* * *

I waited. More time passed. No report. The men and women at Dr. DiMaio's office were obviously having their own problems. Toxicology reports normally take anywhere from two to six weeks. Gary Williams died on March 27th. By the first week in July, the reports had not yet been released.

Dr. DiMaio talked with the district attorney's office several times about the preliminary results. He'd been urged to check his results again. He had. In addition, Dr. Dana had painstakingly checked every initial, every test. She'd checked the chain of evidence to see if indeed they'd conducted the right tests on the right man.

There were no mistakes. It became evident that the public had to be told.

DiMaio runs a tight ship, though, so nothing was getting out prematurely. For two weeks the doctors at the medical examiner's office sat on the information. I kept after it, and was told no one knew anything. The few people I knew at the medical examiner's office said they knew nothing, or they said nothing.

Then, on July 13th I got a telephone call. The findings were in and the news was shocking: Gary Williams had heavy drugs in his blood stream the night he got killed!

The drugs were heroin and cocaine. "Speedballing", is the term most often used to describe the condition where you ingest both of those drugs at once. It is the same ugly drug combination that killed John Belushi.

It was a major story and a major blow to the police department. But, the friend who'd called me to tell me this, also informed me that the story was not going be an exclusive.

He worked for the police department and had found out the news that morning. The Chief of Police was calling a news conference for later that afternoon. He wasn't going to say what it was about, but as a courtesy, my friend thought I should know since I'd broken much of the Hernandez and Williams' stories.

I was being thrown a bone. Nevertheless, I could take comfort in knowing what it was I was scheduled to cover. Since we had no updates and no noon show, I couldn't tell the public. But at least KMOL news knew why I was going to the chief's office at the police department for an afternoon news conference.

It was one of the most crowded news conferences I've ever attended, but, Chief Bill Gibson handled himself masterfully. He promised a full investigation, said he was shocked by the findings, but added that Williams' was considered a loner.

I got back in time for the 5 p.m. news, and threw things together at the last moment:

"Good afternoon, Everyone, I'm Alan Hemberger. Thanks for joining us today," Alan said coming out of the opening credits.

"Shocking news out of the local police department today, as the chief admits an officer who was killed with his own weapon was high on drugs at the time of the murder. Long before Officer Gary Williams was killed on March 27th he had been speedballing, shooting up heroin and cocaine. Brian Karem joins us in the newsroom with the details. Brian?"

"Officer Gary Williams was killed less than four hours into his shift on March 27th. And the next day, Henry David Hernandez and his brother Julian turned themselves into the district attorney to stand trial for that murder. Now on that day we obtained an exclusive interview with Henry David Hernandez and he told us Officer Williams was acting strangely and was enraged the night of the shooting. Today Chief Bill

Gibson said Williams had traces of cocaine and heroin in his blood the day of the shooting."

After I'd introduced the piece, we went to the video tape and an opening comment from Chief Gibson.

"He could have conceivably been injected prior to coming to work because he works the night shift and his death occurred less than halfway through that particular shift," Gibson said.

The district attorney was next on the tape.

"I'm not gonna knee-jerk react right here and say we're not gonna prosecute—no. Because of this new wrinkle we're gonna have to reevaluate. We go the same route, then again we may see that we may have to go straight murder," Fred Rodriquez told the camera. Then, once again the viewers saw and heard me talking from the KMOL newsroom:

"Now the D.A. says the information obviously is bad news for his case. The chief says Williams had left his wife a month prior to his death and was living with a police dispatcher. All of this adds credibility to Hernandez's statement that Williams wasn't playing straight the night of the shooting."

I read over videotape of the shooting scene, then we went into another sound-bite from Henry Hernandez obtained the night he confessed to me:

"It was like as if he was angry. He just wanted to punch somebody and hit them and hit them," Henry said.

By now, I was back on camera:

"The Chief said more than a dozen officers were involved in that investigation over the last several weeks, Alan."

"Brian, have you been able to talk to the Hernandez brothers defense team and what are they saying about this?"

"I talked to both Mark Stevens and Gerry Goldstein late this afternoon. Obviously they are both elated over the news and Goldstein says it should remind everyone to keep in mind that a defendant is innocent until proven guilty."

"Now is this the end of it, or is the investigation still going on, and could it implicate other people?"

"Well the chief says the investigation is pretty much done, although it will remain open and there are reasons for that. Pete Casias, the captain of the northside, said twelve of his men had been interviewed by the chief yesterday. Casias didn't even know of the investigation though, but the chief did not obtain a search warrant for the house where Williams was living, did not ask for drug tests of the officers he investigated, although he could have done so. Finally, the autopsy revealed that Hernandez was correct when he said there was only one gunshot wound . . . a neck wound that the police claimed was a gunshot wound was actually a bite wound as Hernandez had said."

In a little more than two minutes I struggled to put on the air what the newspapers would put into several newspaper articles. Many in the department expressed concern about the autopsy reports, which apparently were available to the chief longer than anyone else since he'd been able to conduct an investigation. Either that, or it was the shortest investigation on record.

Meanwhile Gerry Goldstein mused over what many in the media were thinking.

"If these had been wealthy Anglo northside children, there may have been a different reaction when they accused the department of not acting correctly."

So much for being dead in the water. In the space of a few short days, I suddenly had dozens of leads to look over. That yellow envelope played heavily on my mind. What about the Black Widow? Obviously that was the dispatcher the chief was alluding to in his news conference. What about the investigation into wrongdoing? Where was it going and how far had it gone? What about the dispatch tape? Now the police department's hording of the tape suddenly made sense if there was something to hide. But Gibson didn't impress me as the type to cover something like that up. What was going on?

I began to dive into the chief's news conference for answers. He said that twelve officers had been interrogated on the city's northside nightshift. That's half the officers working dog watch. I needed to talk to, at least, some of them.

As for the drugs, a narcotics agent and a local doctor confirmed that shooting up a quarter of a gram of cocaine and heroin is a common dosage used by addicts. The amount left in Williams' blood stream would be consistent with that, but there was no way to tell for sure because Gary's metabolism, shooting injury, plus blood transfusions he received at the hospital were all variables.

Could blood transfusions or any of his medical treatment be responsible for the drugs in his blood stream? I got a flat, no. Williams had to have been on drugs. For how long, nobody yet knew.

On July 19th I'd gathered enough evidence to go with an additional story. We began with an excerpt from Chief Gibson's news conference.

"He led a rather stable life until a few months ago," the Chief said about Gary Williams. Gibson also said the investigation into Williams' life began nearly a month ago. And according to Gibson, a few months prior to his death, Williams left his wife and the pattern of his life changed dramatically.

"He remained rather aloof. Did not check out for coffee or go out for meals with his fellow officers. And other than that the investigation revealed very little else." Gibson added.

Neighbors however, contradicted some of those facts.

"Several times, we would see police officers; they would come by to his house and eat, or have coffee or take a break or something like that," one neighbor told me.

"So how thorough was the investigation?" I asked on camera. "Neighbors who lived in the same northeast side cul de sac as Williams said he was friendly with them and other police officers, and that on many occasions police would stop by his new home."

This was confirmed by every neighbor who would talk to me. "He was just a good neighbor and a friend. Just like any other neighbor, he would come over and borrow something, or he'd stay or something. He was just a good neighbor, a good man," his next door neighbor confided.

"You would see police officers come and go in there?" I asked this man.

"Yeah. Sure. Not only Gary Williams, but other police officers as well." he repeated.

The neighbors also told us Williams had lived in the cul de sac much longer than police had told us, and more importantly they told us that no members of the Williams' investigation had talked with them.

That certainly seemed interesting. How deep was this investigation?

The police department was saying that at least a

dozen officers had been questioned, but that seemed to be the entire scope of the Williams' investigation.

According to Paul Buske and others closer to the investigation, Williams' girlfriend wasn't questioned very closely and there'd been nothing else done.

And, no one had yet seen or heard the police tape of Williams the night he died. I'd been asking for it for months and had made a request to the attorney general.

Only by mistake, did I find out the attorney general had ruled in my favor. I called the attorney general's office to ask why nothing had been done, and they said something indeed had. They faxed me a copy of the decision, of which copies had been sent to KSAT, but not to me or anyone at KMOL. The police department apparently had not forwarded my original request for the tapes to the state capitol in Austin.

On the 19th I took the fax copy to Paul Buske and he told me he didn't know if the police department could help me.

"I don't know if we can get a copy of it ready for you today. It could be tomorrow," he said. I included this information in my news report that night.

"One of the keys in finding out what happened to Williams that night may be found in what was said between Williams and his dispatcher. KMOL has requested a copy of those tapes, but the police department has denied us access to them. But today the attorney general released this opinion saying those tapes are public record. The police department says it *will* release the tapes, but tomorrow."

I recorded the "stand-up," as we call it in television news, outside the house he shared with his dispatcher girlfriend. She was not home and refused to return any of my telephone calls. Her neighbors said they would tell her, if they saw her, that I wanted to talk to her.

Among some in the department, she was widely suspected of corrupting Gary during his last few months of life. There was a lot of speculation, innuendo, and rumor, but no hard facts. I needed to talk to his girlfriend to get at those facts, but she wasn't cooperative.

Quite the contrary. A few days after the revelation about Gary Williams' drug use became public, Pam got a telephone call at home one night from Gary's girlfriend, known in the police department as the "Black Widow."

I got home late and Pam was still up.

"What's the matter."

"Did you try to contact some woman about a police story you're doing?"

I nodded, "Yes, I did."

"She said she wanted you to stop harassing her or she was going to sue you and the station."

"Great. I haven't even talked to the woman and I'm hassling her . . ."

"She also said to quit talking to her neighbors and other people about her."

"Did she leave a number where I could call."

"No. Did you give her our home number?"

"Of course not."

"Then how did she get our number? It's unlisted."

"What, are you kidding? She's a dispatcher at the police department. She can get any number she wants."

"That's not right."

"Yeah, but what can I do. Did she say anything else?"

"I don't remember, she was pretty threatening and I didn't like it."

"You mean threatening other than threatening to file suite against me?"

"No, but I didn't like her tone, and I told her so."

"What did you say?"

"She started shouting at me that you shouldn't call her and all that stuff and I just told her, look lady he'll call whoever he wants."

"It was more like Pam told her, Look, lady, he'll call whoever in the HELL he DAMN WELL WANTS!" my father told me.

At the end of June my father had left his second wife and at fifty-years-old dropped everything for a chance to start all over again in San Antonio.

His wife, who one of my sisters occasionally referred to as "The Step Monster," must have driven him crazy, because he came to San Antonio without a cent. At first it seemed another little stressful addition to my life.

But, it turned out to be quite advantageous for Pam, Zachary and myself. Dad was always there. And the night Pam got the telephone call, Dad was able to calm her nerves.

"She was pissed-off," he told me. "I've never seen your wife so mad."

The whole Hernandez story was now mushrooming into a personal trial beyond anything I'd ever bargained for. Moreover, my wife, son, and now my father were being dragged into it.

The day after this telephone call, I talked with Larry Macon and Ron Harig about my problem, but there was nothing anyone could do. I chalked it up to experience and decided to go about my business.

On July 20th, that meant, at long last, going over

the Gary Williams dispatch tape. It was more noteworthy for what it didn't have than what it did.

"You know, you made a big mistake by mentioning that on television last night," Buske told me as I came to claim a copy.

"Why is that?"

"Because now every station and newspaper will get a copy. You could have had it by yourself if you hadn't tried to make the department look bad last night. You know part of your problem is that you don't seem to want to do real in-depth reporting."

"I don't?"

"No. It seems you'd rather just make people mad."

I felt like saying, no, I just like to make Paul Buske mad, but I didn't say that. "Well, I appreciate your critique of my reporting style," I said swallowing my anger. "But I just wanted to make sure everyone got the tape."

It was useless to get into a philosophical argument with Buske; so I got the tape and went back to KMOL and studied the case.

The thing most noticeable was that Williams had never called for a backup. A burglar-in-action call usually will bring a call for backup, or a volunteer for a backup, but neither came that night. Or, if it did, it wasn't reflected on the audiotape I'd gotten from the San Antonio Police Department.

There was about a nine-minute gap in between the time Williams got to the Burger Boy, and his next pronouncement that he'd been shot. Then, finally, there was his raspy sigh indicating his great pain as he told his dispatcher that the guys who'd shot him were on the highway, headed westbound.

About a half a dozen of us listened to the tape at KMOL in complete silence. Whatever else you thought of Gary Williams, Henry Hernandez, Julian Hernandez, or any of the legal mess spawned by the stories KMOL had done on the shooting, it always came down to that tape.

You had to hear it to understand. But, for me, Williams' final sigh and pronouncement sounded as final as the slamming of a lid on a coffin.

Chapter 14

Where Do We Go from Here?

Ken Suhler says he always thought Gary Williams would meet an untimely death.

"The saying I've always heard is that one day someone was going to make him eat his night stick," he paused, "and they did."

Suhler says he saw Williams slam his sons up against a car and threaten them. Suhler, a retired military veteran, drove out to meet his sons, at Williams request, after the officer had pulled them over for a traffic violation.

The boys had forgotten their insurance card and license, so the ever helpful father had brought them out to show the police officer. Williams responded, Suhler says, by still threatening to write the kids up for a ticket.

"Hey, what good will this do?" Suhler asked Williams. "Why write these tickets? You're wasting your time, the judge's time and my time, because the tickets are going to be dismissed when I show them these things." He flashed the registration, insurance card, and driver's license.

Williams became enraged.

"I thought the guy was going to shoot me," Suhler later told me. "The guy was a total loser. I don't see how a guy like that could get on the police force."

Suhler's run in with Williams happened nearly a year before the officer's fatal encounter with the Hernandez brothers. I didn't find out about it until after I'd talked to Greg Trimble, following the revelation about Williams' drug test.

Trimble found out from Williams' 201 file, but the information had been unavailable to the media: it wasn't on the public record.

After the report on Williams' drug use surfaced, other things that had been kept quiet about Williams' life began to surface. Following all the leads kept me busy.

Meanwhile, though the State had accused them of committing a crime, the Hernandez brothers were nearly forgotten by the end of the summer. They were swept away in a forgotten jail corner as the more flashy news of a drug using cop took their story's place in the tabloids.

Although Henry and Julian passed this time in the monotonous confines of the Bexar County Jail, each handled jail differently.

Henry's "dark side" as a prison guard had once called it, continued spreading. He continued to spend his time making friends with the Mexican Mafia. Since he was accused of killing a cop, and had admitted as much on television, he had the credentials to join. The prison gang is a brotherhood—a way of life. You do as your superiors tell you. You establish loyalties and protect those in the brotherhood. You kill who you're told to kill.

If it sounds familiar, it is. Almost every other organized crime gang has similar customs. The Mexican Mafia is no different than the Italian Mafia and probably just as dangerous—at least to its own members.

During the last five years there has been bloody and massive violence within the ranks of the members of the Mexican Mafia as power struggle after power struggle leads to death.

There've been several cases of bodies found on the side of the road, shot to death in the Alazan Apache Courts and other housing projects and then deposited on some vacant, forgotten road in the city or county.

One body was found out by Loop 1604 and Interstate 10. As a patrolman approached he could see what appeared to be the body of a man in his midfifties. His legs and arms had been bound behind his back. He was found on two knees leaning against a fence post, his pants pulled down to his knees and his head a thick clot of drying blood.

As the deputy went to turn the head around, the man suddenly spoke, "Get the hell off me you sonovabitch," the seemingly dead man snarled.

It turned out to be an aging member of the Mexican Mafia whose underlings had decided to grab some power for themselves. They'd brought the man out to a remote location and shot him in the back of the head with a 9mm semi-automatic pistol. But, the two young gang members apparently didn't know how to aim a pistol properly at the back of someone's head. The bullet merely grazed the scalp and knocked their mentor unconscious.

"Even the Mexican Mafia can't get good help these days," Sheriff Harlon Copeland declared.

"There's going to be some blood shed tonight. You can count on that."

Of course, most of the Mafia's victims are not so fortunate. The burglaries, robberies and assaults committed by gang members touch hundreds if not thousands of innocent victims every year.

Henry, unable to function in a larger society, sought a group where he could belong, a group he understood and a group that understood him. In all, his choices were limited. The Mafia seemed to fit his needs best.

When I heard that Henry was becoming involved in the Mexican Mafia, I began researching gangs in San Antonio. A few weeks later, I put together the first KMOL story on the Mexican Mafia. Shortly thereafter, I found that San Antonio not only had a prison gang problem, but a street gang problem as well.

The San Antonio police would deny it for two years, before a gang shooting at a local high school punctured that fantasy and left the department facing an uncertain reality.

While Henry was finding one way to survive in jail, Julian found another. Tom Barry referred to him as a "model prisoner." He joined the general jail population and had even been granted status as a trustee which meant he could work outside his cell—a rare status indeed for a man who stood accused of killing a cop.

According to Greg Trimble, Julian's family continued to hope he would turn his life around. Julian showed no signs in jail of betraying that trust.

Meanwhile, I was hunting down cops who'd been close to Gary Williams. Cris Anders, a friend of Gary's and a fellow officer, told me that Gary had once been a rodeo clown and was just a "good ole boy". He was shocked when he found out Williams had drugs in his bloodstream the night he was gunned down.

Cris had been one of the twelve who'd been questioned by the police department's Internal Affairs Division after Williams' drug use became public.

"It was shocking," Cris told us. "Gary was just this real straight arrow for so long. We went through cadet class together. He was a family man; then he left his wife and took up with a dispatcher," he told me.

"The Black Widow," I said.

"Yeah." He cocked his head, "Where'd you hear that name?"

"I thought that was commonly known nickname in the department," I replied. Police nicknames, although not usually imaginative, do tend to stick.

Cris told me, "You hear all kinds of rumors about her and Gary."

He went through the most common ones for me again, and added a few that I hadn't heard. But, the stories still remained unsubstantiated rumors. Cris could not confirm anything, despite being a close friend of Gary's. Like everyone else, he'd just "heard something from someone."

Despite Cris' lack of affection for Gary's last romantic partner, he remained defensive of Gary's flight from his marriage.

"Well, you can't really blame Gary. I mean he went through hell with his wife. She became born again or something and Gary said he hadn't had a piece of ass at home for close to three years."

"Well, that's certainly enough to drive a man insane," I said in an ironic tone, half under my breath.

He picked up the remark. "Exactly," he said, nodding.

I think he missed the intended sarcasm. But, then again, maybe not.

Over the next few months, I probably talked to more than fifty cops who'd either worked with Gary or knew him. Many thought him a quiet conscientious policeman and were shocked that Gary had been on drugs the night of his death. Others called him a "bumpkin" or "good ole boy," and nodded knowingly.

Meanwhile, some of Williams' former neighbors with whom I also talked, actually seemed relieved to hear the news of Gary's use of drugs.

"At least it explains why he was acting so differently lately," one of them told me.

I was beginning to think there were two Gary Williams.

In an effort to clarify the situation, I telephoned Greg Trimble, Mark Stevens' private investigator, and taking advantage of our previous relationship, tried to find out if he knew anything that I should look into.

Knowing he was Steven's investigator, I was sure anything he gave me would not be in the best interest of the State's case, but I had other sources for that side of the story.

Greg, one of those perpetual Democratic worker bees has an ability to survive that few have matched. He has toiled away at a lot of different jobs, but was always right in there, wherever the action was.

He got into the Hernandez case reluctantly, but now was feeling his oats ferreting out corruption in the police department.

"There are a couple of things you might look into," he told me one day. "But none of this you got from me."

"Sure," I said.

"I think I can trust you there, you already went to jail once for shielding your source."

"Twice," I corrected him. "And I have no desire to go there a third time."

"I just don't want Mark to know, until after the trial, that I gave you anything."

"Sure. It's all right with me. But, if he starts getting too pushy, you may have to set him straight. I don't think he'd like it too much if I was forced in open court to name his own investigator as a source for a story. It wouldn't look too good for either one of you." Since my jailing, I'd been much more exact in what it was I would promise sources, and I had no intention of going to jail to protect Mark Stevens. Not after the grueling ordeal he'd help put me through.

"Yeah, okay," he said.

I guess it didn't matter to him what I said, because he still furnished me with information.

"Have you looked at his 201 file?" he asked.

The police department's 201 file is the personnel file kept on every officer. It lists suspensions, promotions, and anything else pertinent to an officer's career.

Greg handed me Gary's 201 file. I was surprised. I didn't know there were things in an officer's 201 file that weren't part of the public record. As it turned out, Greg had gotten ten copies of complaints, letters, and other material pertinent to the case that the police department never made available to the public. It was this type of information that I sorely needed to put together a better picture of Gary Williams.

Then Greg dropped a minor bomb shell on me. It turned out, he had much more information about Gary's drug problem than anyone else had been able to track down—including the police department, that is if you believed what the police department was telling the public.

"Did you know I found someone who says he sold drugs to Williams?" Greg asked me.

Now, that did make my hair stand at attention.

"What do you mean? Are you sure?"

"That's what the guy says."

"Do you believe him?"

"The question is, will a jury believe him. He's in jail right now, so who knows?"

I thought of using the guy myself, until Greg mentioned he was in jail. Still, it might be worth something. I decided to take a chance.

While we were talking, I invited Greg down to KMOL to tell me more. He accepted.

We met in the news department's conference room—a large, glassed-in enclosure just near my desk that serves a variety of purposes. I wasn't taking any chances. I didn't want to meet him in any darkened garage at midnight.

I still didn't know whether or not to trust Greg. I liked him, but maybe Mark Stevens was trying to set me up. I wanted a lot of people in KMOL's newsroom to see us together. It might not have been complete protection, but it sure felt good to me.

"Please sit down," I pointed to a chair.

"How was jail?" he said smiling.

"Better than the courtroom," I answered.

Greg leaned towards me, "There's a lot you need to know," he said ominously. After listening to him for a few minutes, I decided that he might just have something. I excused myself, went back to my desk and dug out some of the stuff I'd been working on.

I handed him a piece of paper with a former police officer's name on it. He'd quit the force, left town, and was nowhere to be seen. It was rumored that, at one point, he had been dating Sue Carter, the so called, "Black Widow". According to a friend of mine at the department, she also was suspected of supplying drugs. Perhaps to Gary Williams.

Greg had never heard of him. But, he told me he'd heard some other interesting things.

My ears perked up. The allegations and rumors involving Gary Williams' real character and behavior were quickly gaining momentum.

David Elizondo, one of the police reporters at the *San Antonio Light* had heard many of the same things I had.

We sat one night in the SAPD press room and discussed the options.

"I've heard the same thing, dude," he said. "But I think it's just talk. Nobody has any proof."

Not yet, but suddenly, within a space of a few short weeks, I had two thick files dedicated to further developments in the Williams' case. Yet, it was next to impossible to separate the wheat from the chaff. I had a lot of information, yes, but so far I'd only been able to do one story on the issue—a piece that looked at how police brass deal with corruption—not very meaty stuff.

Finally, I decided I had to trust someone. I phoned the local head of the Drug Enforcement Administration, Vernon Parker, and sounded him out.

Vernon, a perpetual straight arrow who relishes the thought of busting crooked cops, had heard some of what I told him. He was interested and wanted more.

I faced a dilemma. I didn't want to tell him enough to destroy my chances of a story. But I had to tell him enough that he could better check what I had found out.

Before I could meet in person with Vernon though, I had to go back to court.

* * *

On Wednesday, September 13th, I entered a courtroom adjacent to the state capital, where a skeptical majority of the Court of Criminal Appeals peppered Bexar County Prosecutor Ed Shaughnessy with acid comments about Judge James Barlow's authority to toss me in jail twice.

Suppressing a smile, I sat back. Finally, it appeared, things were going KMOL's way.

Larry Macon didn't see it my way.

"If we're going to win this, we'll win this on a technicality," Larry Macon said. "Barlow did not have the case assigned to him in court and technically he had no authority to throw you in jail."

"Wonderful."

"Exactly right."

"Couldn't someone have caught this before I went to jail twice?"

"We all missed it."

In chambers Macon made his point again. "There was no legal basis" for tossing me in jail, and that confidential sources were essential to news gathering.

Under Texas law it seemed rather clear cut that Barlow did not really have the authority to throw me in jail since the Hernandez brothers were not indicted for Williams' murder at the time and the case wasn't assigned to Barlow's court.

Meanwhile, Shaughnessy argued that "Members of the news media, whoever they might be, do not have any specialized privileges in withholding information."

The nine-member panel seemed to take it all in stride, but at one point, Judge Marvin O. Teague, one of the court's more outspoken members could no longer hold his real feelings in.

"I'm at a loss here about Judge Barlow, or 'God'

Barlow, whatever you want to call him. What was before him at the time?" Teague mused.

"I think if Judge Barlow had his way, he'd be God Barlow," Shaughnessy shot back.

Teague also wanted to know why Barlow wanted my notes, "other than to be nosy." Macon said Barlow never really made that point clear.

The court took the case under advisement. It could be a week, it could be a year before they decided.

But, I left feeling happier than I had in a while. Clearly, I said, "the court will eventually rule in our favor."

Again, Macon expressed some ambivalence.

"They might," Macon explained. "But by the way most of the questioning was going, it looks like they will rule on a very narrow point. They'll throw the things out on a technicality and we'll have to go through all of this again when the Hernandez brothers go to trial."

When was my ordeal going to end?

Apparently not soon enough. I stayed out of the news for the rest of the year and got to spend Christmas with my family. But, by the first part of 1990, the case had been reassigned to Judge Pat Priest's court.

The Court of Criminal Appeals still hadn't ruled on Barlow's old order when I found out from Macon that Priest was setting a hearing for early February. Once again I'd be put on the witness stand.

I was now looking at the distinct possibility of being tossed in jail a third time by a second judge.

"I wonder if that's some kind of record?" Sharon Adams mused one day in the newsroom.

A few weeks later Beth Taylor finally got the Hernandez brothers indicted. She did it without my testimony which she so desperately said she had to have, and all the parties involved got ready for round three.

Chapter 15

Further News

While I tried to gather more evidence on the San Antonio's police department and Gary Williams' use of drugs, KMOL began going through some typical, but none-the-less, upsetting television upheavals. Ron had decided to change the look and take a lunge at the First Place ratings brass ring held by KENS-TV.

Lori Tucker, our lead female anchor was the first to fall victim to the hatchet.

I stood talking with her husband and photographer, Steve Wiggins, in the newsroom one afternoon as she walked into Ron's office. All the offices are lined in glass, much like the cages you see at the zoo. While inside, we couldn't hear much, but Lori's waving hands and wild gesticulations certainly caught our attention.

Moments later, she stormed out of Ron's office.

"I'll never break air at this station again!" she screamed.

I was wondering if she was swearing off flatulence when she grabbed a box and began throwing her belongings inside. Apparently she meant something different. She didn't want to talk about it though, so she grabbed her stuff and left.

As this was after the five o'clock newscast, there were few people around. Lori's coanchor Alan Hemberger came back moments later from dinner and found out Lori had been given a six-month notice that the station was not going to renew her contract. She stormed off madder than hell and quit.

I'd been witness to most of this, but, of course, I didn't find out the whole story behind it until Jeanne Jakle told us in her column the next morning.

On the one hand, I felt sorry for Lori that she'd been given the sack, but on the other hand, I'd been canned before and no one had ever been nice enough to give me six months notice.

Alan soloed for a while as an anchor, but soon management gave him the sack too.

Alan, who'd also anchored and reported for *Entertainment Tonight* before coming back to KMOL, landed on his feet and is now anchoring at the number one station in Houston. Lori is anchoring for an independent station there.

Then, there was Suzanne Wolffe. The short, fireplug of a woman with the omnipresent cigarette was given the sack too. She had a great Gilbert Godfried way about her that was going to make her hard to replace—well, strictly on a personal level anyway.

She, myself, and a crew of reporters, photographers and editing equipment made their way down to the Texas Coast to cover hurricane Gilbert before she left.

Forever frozen in my mind is my memory of her covering the Big Storm from one of the last hotels left open.

At the time KMOL didn't have a Satellite Truck which would enable us to go "Live" from anywhere on the planet. So, we had to borrow, beg, and buy

Satellite time from other NBC affiliates, or anyone else with a Satellite Truck, for our newscast.

We'd found a station out of Oklahoma City willing to sell us time, but Suzanne had been told that the Satellite Truck was new and the station wasn't going to risk bringing it to the coast. The expensive toy could get ripped to shreds by hurricane winds. So, it was parked miles away in Alice, Texas. If we wanted to go live, we had to drive there.

With *2001 A Space Odyssey* playing on the television set behind her, Suzanne walked up to me, burning cigarette in hand, and squared off. She pointed at me with the cigarette butt while adjusting her deep rimmed glasses with the other hand.

"They want us to go to Alice, Texas for a live-shot. Christ. What the hell could ever happen in Alice Texas?"

I had no idea, but felt I was supposed to quickly find a copy of an encyclopedia that could tell us.

KMOL ended up happening in Alice, Texas. It was a low spot for all concerned. The Satellite truck was parked in a parking lot of the low-rent hotel. There were a few clouds in the sky, no wind to speak of, and in the background of the live-shot you could see 18-wheelers pulling in and out of the parking lot. Every once in a while one of the drivers would honk, so we all would know that he knew he was on television.

One proud moment came when a weather man from somewhere down in Alabama jumped in front of the camera for his turn to talk to the folks back home via-Satellite. As he did so, a camera hungry cricket jumped on him and proceeded to walk from shoulder to shoulder as the man calmly explained that even though it wasn't windy now, boy that big old hurricane was just bearing down on us.

Another shining moment arrived when the Oklahoma City crew showed up with their anchors dressed in yellow rain slickers so they could do the news in the dry weather of Alice, Texas.

And Suzanne topped it all off.

"Ch-Rist," Suzanne made it a two syllable word. "Thank God this ain't brain surgery!"

To replace Lori and Alan, KMOL hired Debora Daniels from the second-rated ABC affiliate down the street, and according to Jeanne Jakle, paid her something to the tune of $1.1 million over the next five years to perform her reading duties two times a night, five days a week.

They replaced Suzanne with Forrest Carr, a former KMOL producer who'd gone on to Tampa as a producer there.

These upheavals led to problems covering the Gary Williams' story. While Alan Hemberger seemed alert, interested, and encouraging in the pursuit of the story, our new anchor, who'd watched most of it from a distance at our competitor station, seemed aloof and uncaring.

Moreover, I had to bring Forrest and new reporters up to speed on the story as the weeks and months rolled on. Each time another development occurred, Ron and I would stop and go over the story's history for the new kids on the block.

Continuity was a problem that took several months to conquer. I'm not sure we ever did it adequately. At one point Forrest Carr told Larry Macon that he could "understand why people didn't want to protect the media's First Amendment rights. We don't really need them anyway."

"Well, you won't be the first witness we'll call on our behalf," Larry and I countered. Despite his early skepticism, Forrest later surprised me by coming through for me.

But, in the beginning, the new people on staff caused more problems than they helped to solve. The station upheaval also occurred at the worst time. We were preparing for court again. As 1990 kicked off, with round three ready to take place in a new courtroom in front of a new judge, and with all the new people on our staff, I was more nervous than I'd been since Gary Williams got shot and I'd gotten the interview with Henry Hernandez.

All these changes slowed down my fact gathering and stymied my investigation. My frustration mounted.

But one phone call changed all that.

The caller, a police officer whose voice I immediately recognized, announced: "Gary Williams was not the only one."

Reeling from that shock I asked, "What do you mean?"

Then he told me, "There weren't many officers involved, but some had gotten together and were supplying narcotics to officers who used drugs. Certain establishments were used as bases for the operation."

Hanging up, I tried to determine the information's validity. There was always the possibility I was being fed a line of bullshit, but it had the smell of truth.

Within days, I found another person had heard similar stories. Cynthia Orr, at Gerald Goldstein's office, had even heard of a nickname given to a pack of drug dealing patrolmen who'd supposedly been operating on the city's northwest side.

As we discussed our findings, we found that sharing information could be mutually beneficial to both of us—although she stopped short of telling me anything that might compromise Julian Hernandez's case, and I stopped short of telling her anything I felt would betray my sources' confidence.

Further pursuing this new development lead, I called Vernon Parker at the D.E.A. This time I was determined to set up a meeting. He said I needed Police Chief Bill Gibson there too. I agreed.

I met the two men in Vernon's office. I was nervous. Ethically I had responsibilities to those who'd provided me information. But, I hadn't been able to develop a story with the information either. I couldn't even confirm that what I had was legitimate. I wasn't going to give anything up that would compromise anyone who talked to me, but I also felt a civic duty to let someone know what was going on. Besides, I thought, if Vernon and the chief already knew what I was about to tell them, then maybe they'd spill something to me.

The three of us sat down and I sketched out the information I had for them. It wasn't a whole lot, but I did have some names, some possible times, and a possible method of operation. "I don't have enough for a story," I told him, "but if I do, I'll break it." Gibson said he understood. I also told him that if his investigation led to anything, then I would want to know about it ahead of anyone else in the media. He agreed, and told me to work closely with one of his intelligence officers.

"I'm not going to ask you who told you this," Chief Gibson continued. "But, I want you to be careful."

"Don't get caught doing anything illegal," Parker explained. If this guy is caught up in it and he wants you along you could be in trouble."

This much I knew. But, it was nice to hear their concern. "That's one of the reasons why I brought this to you," I told both men. "I've been unable to develop a story on it or substantiate anything. If it's a crock, then fine. But, if this turns out to be something, well I'd like something done and I'd like a story out of it."

The Chief agreed and told me to contact Frank Castillon, from the department's intelligence division. Any further information I was to give directly to him. I knew Frank, but not that well.

"Do you trust him?"

"Yes," the chief answered. "Anything you tell him will stay with him."

I met with Frank one afternoon at a small city park I didn't know existed. We sat in the hot February San Antonio sun and I outlined for him the things I'd previously told the chief and Vernon Parker. Frank, of course, wanted to know who my source was, I told him I couldn't tell him. He respected that.

"I have to do the same thing sometimes," he told me. "If it came down to compromising a source in court, I couldn't do it."

We proceeded to talk, and Frank said he believed he knew who my source was, but again I repeated, "I can't tell you." What I found interesting, though, was that Frank was hearing almost the exact same rumors I was. In fact, some of the same officers I'd been checking out, he'd been investigating.

Frank also told me he'd heard Gary's name connected to some of the things I'd been looking into and that the department had thoroughly gone over those allegations—with no results yet.

Apparently, the Chief's investigation into Gary Williams' death went much deeper than the chief or anyone else in the department cared to let on. That was encouraging in one sense, because I felt the shoddy workup on the Williams' case was one reason not to trust the police department with the information I'd obtained. DEA was much more professional and thorough, in my opinion. But, as it turned out, the police had not been entirely candid about what they'd done. At least, according to Frank, they'd done a lot more investigating than anyone had previously disclosed.

I shouldn't have been surprised, but I was. I didn't think that type of subterfuge was possible by S.A.P.D.

Chapter 16

I Won't Back Down . . .

As the court battle and the Williams' story spun on, some interesting side effects associated with the story cropped up.

The strangest of these were the anonymous telephone tips I began getting at work. Despite the fact that when his death was announced, no one would talk about Gary Williams, everyone, it seemed knew something about him. And now, since I'd been so willing to protect my sources, they seemed to feel I could be trusted with grave secrets that many had been afraid to tell anyone before.

Many of these "secrets" were offered to me by what many term "coconuts" and I became immediately suspicious whenever anyone told me that they had to share this information with me because the chief of police, the F.B.I., and the D.E.A. couldn't be trusted.

Some of these tips were just plain silly, such as the woman who called up claiming to know that Gary Williams was still alive and the shooting had been a plot to hide S.A.P.D. drug dealing and gambling. After that story which didn't make sense, I was curious as to whether or not I'd suddenly be hit with a rash of Gary Williams' sightings. I was waiting for the call that placed Gary at a neighborhood Burger King having lunch with Elvis. That call never came. It was about the only one I didn't get.

I did, however, receive a variety of calls from those who claimed Gary was actually gunned down by a fellow cop, or that Gary had taken his own life. One fellow called and excitedly told me that Gary and the Hernandez brothers were actually undercover D.E.A. agents and he knew because he saw the exact same story on an episode of *Miami Vice*.

Because of these assorted absurdities, I began wondering about every caller who phoned me—even contacts I trusted and knew were giving me valuable information.

So it was no wonder I felt odd about a call I got at the station just prior to my February court appearance.

It was Greg Trimble again. In a cloak and dagger type of whisper, he said he had to come over and talk to me about something extremely important.

"You got some free time tonight, brother?" he asked.

I was knee-deep in the business of putting a story together for the 5 P.M. newscast, but I couldn't resist.

"Yeah, Greg, I got some time after the newscast. You wanna talk?"

"Yeah, you gonna be at the station?"

"Sure. Meet me here. What do you wanna talk about?"

"I can't tell you right now. But, I'll let you know when I get there."

He hung up. I hung up. I couldn't help thinking

the call seemed rather strange. Still I hadn't talked to Greg in a while; maybe he'd come up with a tip I could use. Then again, maybe he wanted to blow smoke up my pants. Who knew.

Shortly before 7 P.M., he knocked at the station's back door. Somebody let him in and he walked over to my desk.

"Hey, Greg, what's up?"

He smiled. "Nothing much. Can we talk someplace?"

The conference room was full; so I motioned him towards an edit bay. I closed the door.

"What's up, Greg? What's going on?"

He pulled out a piece of paper. "Sorry brother. I have to do this."

I looked. It was a subpoena. I almost laughed. I had at least a half a dozen others sitting on my desk.

"Greg, why the cloak-and-dagger? You didn't actually think I'd try to dodge a subpoena? Besides, I've already got enough subpoenas to paper my walls."

"I had to do it. Mark wanted to make sure you'd be in court. He wanted this done today. I'd put it off for as long as I could."

"Well, tell Mark Stevens I can't wait to have the pleasure of his company in district court."

I signed the subpoena showing that I'd been served. It was hard to hold back a laugh.

I wish I could say the rest of February turned out to be fun, but unfortunately it didn't. In fact, my date in court with a brand new judge turned out to be dead serious.

Judge Pat Priest is a short, fire plug of a man who looks like he'd be hell in a boxing ring. And, while he was fair, he was definitely not interested in protecting the press. I doubt if witnesses, juries, attorneys, or the accused would have much luck intimidating the man.

Larry Macon found that out the hard way during what would be my worst trip to court in February of 1990.

Larry Macon was out to try our case in the press and did everything he could to put pressure on Judge Pat Priest to let me go. Priest didn't like that, nor did he like Macon's accusations that Judge Priest was not doing the right thing.

Larry walked into court during one of my hearings, grinning and laughing as he usually does. Priest caught him with a perturbed glare that spelled doom.

"I don't like what you had to say on television," the judge said before the official start of the hearing.

Larry answered something to the effect that the judge would get over it.

I grimaced. It was easy to see that I might be placed in the middle of an obvious personality conflict.

Ron, sitting next to me in court, turned and said in his low key whisper, "Oh great."

The Larry Macon/Pat Priest personality conflict wasn't the only one aired in court. Beth Taylor and I squared off in a high pitched shouting match that made us sound like something from the Honeymooners.

She tried to back me into a corner during her cross examination. I had written an article in a local magazine about my feelings toward the First Amendment and why I felt it was necessary to keep my sources confidential.

Taylor read a passage where I said that without the First Amendment, the entire house of cards would tumble, and I had no intention of letting that happen.

I Won't Back Down . . . 187

"Do you still feel that way," she said with a sly grin.

I did. As I answered that, with a magician's sleight of hand she produced a tape. Months before I had talked with Jim Holguin; Taylor had the tape, even though Holguin had sworn he'd turned his recorder off.

Now she played it in front of the court so everyone could hear my terrible acting attempt at getting the dispatcher tape from the police department.

I sat calmly through it and tried to grin back. It was hard to match the hypnotic stare levelled at me, but I gave it my best shot.

At one point in time in our conversation, I'd mentioned to him that I had the tapes, they were under my desk locked away in a safe place. I urged him to subpoena us because the tapes would be gone in a week and we could use that as a defense against producing them.

Clearly, I'd gone too far in trying to coax information out of Holguin, but it was equally clear Taylor mistook my conversation for something else.

"So where are those tapes now?" she said intimidatingly.

"You have them."

We loudly argued about that for a moment.

Her voice rose venomously, "What about this conversation with Jimmy Holguin on March 29, 1989; were you lying to him when you said you had them?"

At the end, she was screaming so loud and at such a high pitch, I was sure my silver fillings were vibrating.

"Oh my goodness!" I put my hands to my face to mock her. Then said with disgust, "No, ma'am I'm not lying, and I don't appreciate your tone."

Still, she kept after me trying to insinuate that I

had kept tapes from the district attorney and that somewhere there existed a complete version of the conversation I had with Hernandez.

That day Taylor tried to accuse Ron of lying, me of lying, and possibly our attorney of lying, as if we'd cooked up some scheme to keep vital information from Beth Taylor.

"So you lied here?" she yelled, her eyes livid with anger.

"I didn't say I lied. No."

She yelled louder, "Which is it? Did you lie here . . . ?"

Macon jumped up. He'd had enough and began yelling, "Excuse me, Your Honor."

"Sit down." The judge yelled back. I looked over at him, he was staring at Larry Macon with a look of pure contempt on his face. I swallowed hard.

"Your Honor," Larry continued. "I would like that . . ."

"Sit down!" Judge Priest's voice thundered. Then he looked at me. "Answer the question."

I moved my mouth to speak, but Larry was quicker. He had no intention of being bullied nor intimidated.

"I do have a right to make an objection!" Larry's face was now red.

"Yes, and it's overruled. Sit down!" the judge bellowed. The personal animosity between the two men was now erupting on the surface.

"I have a right to make it." Larry would not bend.

"Make it," Priest snapped.

"I'm making it. She is yelling at the witness. It's unfair . . ."

"It is overruled. Please be seated."

Priest leveled a stony glare at Beth Taylor who

was uncharacteristically silent. "Ask the question." He spit it out.

"Thank you, Your Honor." Macon grinned as he left that parting shot. Then he sat down.

Beth had quieted down a little, and I was at a loss for words. I stole a glance at the Judge and then at Macon. Under different circumstances I was sure the two would have gone at each other with fists flying.

"Did you lie in this cassette that we've just heard . . ." Beth sneered.

That snapped me back. "About what?" I said, unsure of her meaning.

"Or," she said accusingly, "did you lie to Jimmy Holguin about secreting audio cassette tapes that . . ."

"No, if you . . ." I tried to explain.

"Listen to my question first." Beth was dead calm. I stopped.

"I'm sorry."

". . . that you used what you recorded with Henry David Hernandez?"

I thought I knew what she meant; so I tried to answer.

"Okay. You're just mistaking what we're saying. What I told Jimmy is what I'm telling you now. We had those tapes. They were in my desk. I gave them to you. When we searched diligently for those tapes, that's what we found. Now, whether you want to call them audio, or you want to call them video, or if you want to call them anything. What we had left was what was in my desk. That's what we found. That's what we gave."

Beth exploded again. "You searched diligently and lo and behold, by God, you found them in your desk?"

"No, ma'am." I tried to remain calm, but Beth was unrelenting and didn't seem to get my point.

"Is that what you're telling us?"

"No." I said. "That's where I put them. I told him I put them in my desk after I found them and that's where they were."

Beth winced. "I have no more questions." Perhaps she finally caught on.

By the end of the day the Judge was convinced KMOL had turned over all the tapes we had, despite the screaming sideshow. But, he wasn't prepared to bend on anything else. He'd dissolved the old order that Barlow had issued which found me in contempt of court, but he made it quite plain that I was going to suffer the same fate again.

As I got off the witness stand, I made my way past Mark Stevens.

"That was certainly interesting Mark. Having my thumbs screwed to the wall would only be marginally more fun."

"You did pretty well up there. You didn't crack."

"Like that was ever an option."

I left the courtroom to another barrage of questions by reporters. Meanwhile, a telephone call to my newsroom let me know it was in a state of frenzy. Forrest Carr was going nuts because Carol Cavazos, who at the time was our courthouse reporter, said that Beth Taylor had destroyed me when she pulled out the tape between me and Jimmy Holguin.

Ron and Forrest became convinced we were going to "take a bath" in the local press on the tape. They were extremely worried. Ron, Larry and I talked about it.

"I thought you sold us out with that tape, Brian," Ron told me.

"Ron, I'm not a sleazy person," I said. "I think

you sold me out a long time ago. You haven't been behind this effort from the first day."

"And I think this proves I'm right. This is not a case to go to the wall for."

Perhaps he was correct in a sense, but, of course, now it was too late. And, I had no reason nor inclination to air all my own private reservations. I made a decision to protect someone. Come hell or jail I was going to do it.

Macon strove to get us back on track.

"We can argue about this later. Brian, I think you lost some credibility earlier, but you got it back. The question is, what do we do now?"

Ron was still reticent to go forward.

"Jesus, Larry, if I go in there and give up those notes now, then I'm as sleazy as Beth Taylor tried to convince everyone I was. Yeah, I made a mistake in trying to shmooze Jimmy Holguin. But, I'm not going to compound that mistake by making a bigger one by giving them the notes."

"Have you been able to get in touch with your source at all?"

"No. Plus I don't want to let the likes of Beth Taylor, Mark Stevens, or even Gerry Goldstein intimidate me."

"I agree with you on that, Brian," Larry said. "I just want to make sure we're all together on this."

We looked at Ron. If he said no, I'd split from KMOL right then and ask Larry to continue on my behalf. But Ron nodded in the affirmative. I breathed a sigh of relief.

My faith in Ron had wavered as I'm sure his faith in me had. But both of us remained committed to doing the right thing. We walked back inside the courtroom and got the bad news. Judge Pat Priest was giving me the night to think about giving up my evidence.

Although Barlow's old order was dissolved, if I didn't give in and turn over my notebook and sources by the following day, Priest said he'd reissue the order.

We left. I can barely remember walking down the steps of the courthouse and going home.

That night Pam and I decided to go to the weekly meeting of the San Antonio Press Club at the Cadillac Bar. The club is strictly social and gathers once a week over cheap drinks to gripe about work and the decline of Western civilization.

I was convinced it would be my last free night in a while and we both decided it would be a good idea to get out and spend the time with friends. Staying home was too gloomy. We'd put Zachary to bed, and neither one of us wanted to stew over the possibilities that the next day might bring, so we called our sitter.

Apparently we weren't the only ones who thought I was staring at my last night of freedom in at least six months. Michelle Salcedo, who was covering the story for the *San Antonio Light*, met with us over cocktails and tried to console us.

"You all prepared?" she asked us.

Pam smiled, nodded. "I guess as much as we'll ever be."

"I don't know what else to do to prepare," I said. "I've been through this twice before. It's starting to get to be old hat. I just wish whatever would happen, would happen. I just want to get it over with."

The conversation drifted back and forth over a couple of drinks, and I found myself having to ask a question about what Michelle thought about the Holguin tape.

"Ah, hell, most of us know a good reporter would do anything to get a story. Don't worry about it. You're doing the right thing." I breathed a heavy sigh.

"Thanks, to tell the truth, I don't know what to think any more—or whom to trust."

It was no wonder. People who Pam and I had known for years, friends I'd worked with, were suddenly peppering Pam with questions, trying to get the inside track on what was going on.

Pam simply quit returning telephone calls to anyone we knew in the media.

The next morning, February 9, 1990, all the parties involved in the story gathered once again inside Judge Priest's chambers.

"Do you intend to produce the items that you were ordered to produce?" Priest asked me.

I looked straight at him, my emotions surging under the surface while I tried to keep my voice calm.

"Well, Your Honor, I thought about it a lot overnight, and a lot of things happened yesterday, and a lot of things were said, but what it all comes down to is I made a promise to some people—and you all have your job to do and I have my job to do. I'm sorry that I cannot, Your Honor, but I did make a promise and I intend to keep my promise."

He held my gaze. "All right, sir. Then I do, as I feel I must, hold that you are in contempt of the Court for failure to follow that order . . . I order that you be fined five hundred dollars and confined for a period of six months, or until you have purged yourself of contempt by producing to this Court the notes you were ordered to produce."

Priest, though, showed himself to be humane. He arranged for me to stay in his office, while Macon attempted to arrange for an appeal.

Since I didn't think this was a possibility, I was convinced I would soon be making my home at the Bexar County Jail.

By lunchtime, apparently Pat Priest had come to the same conclusion. As everyone adjourned for lunch, I was shipped downstairs to the new holding cells in the new Bexar County Justice Center.

This was going to be my third trip to jail. I sat on cold steel, munching an apple and a bologna sandwich which the jail had sent over for lunch. My only companion in a freezing air conditioned cell that could hold thirty men easily, was a fifty-five-year-old man named Roberto.

He sported several prison tatoos and wore the orange jail togs that meant he was a semi-permanent resident of the jail. Naturally we struck up a conversation and, of course, I asked him why he was in jail.

"I had a disagreement with my old lady," he told me. "The district attorney says I shot her, man."

"Wonderful," came my reply.

"Hey man, it was just my old lady. I ain't never shot a man before."

Imagine how soundly we'd all sleep knowing that.

A few hours later, Macon surprised me once again and got me out while we once again continued the appeal. As it turns out, the State did take another look at our case, so once again we were before the criminal court of appeals and once again I was out, free, and appealing—the case. Me and yo-yo's were beginning to have a lot in common.

Meanwhile, Mark Stevens was keeping Greg Trimble up to date on the Williams' case. On February 14, he sent a letter to Greg that stated two days before, "Judge Priest turned over certain documents to us regarding internal affairs investigations of Gary Lee Williams."

Mark outlined the two cases against Williams in

his 201 file and noted that one man claimed Williams was "surly, petulant and belligerent."

Mark also said that one of the cases, "could be very significant because of the similarity of our case."

Cynthia Orr, from Mark Goldstein's office had also gone over Williams 201 file and noted that one of the cases looked to have more credible witnesses, while the other she noted as "interesting" because "Williams called off his cover here as in our case."

The lawyers were building their fire to show that Williams had a history of abusive behavior. But only two cases in his 201 file for the entire time Williams served on the force did not seem to build up a real strong argument that Williams was a bully.

That kept me from doing more stories about Williams. I felt I needed more.

So, I began pouring over months of notes again, and came across the February 5, 1987, *San Antonio Express-News*. An article on the inside of the Metro section noted that a police officer "preparing to join" in a chase of juvenile auto theft suspects had overturned his police car and the car skidded some one hundred feet on its top. The wreck injured the officer inside who was sent to Northeast Baptist Hospital. The officer was Gary Williams. This turned out to be the same incident that Paul Thompson had talked to me about and the same article he'd referred me to weeks ago. I'd forgotten it in all my court hassles.

Williams apparently received very minor injuries in the crash, and the whole incident would have meant little, if it were not for the apparent fact that Williams was miles away from the chase when he turned his car over!

I decided to investigate further and found out the chase actually began in the small bedroom community of Universal City which is North of San Antonio, just off of Interstate 35. Williams overturned his car, according to reports, in the 11400 block of Perrein Beitel.

After obtaining the police reports from the department, and looking at old newspaper reports, I checked to see whether we had any video of the accident.

In the old files, I found it. I scrutinized the shot Daffy must have taken of the upside down cruiser and tried to pinpoint the exact location on Perrein Beitel.

On a cool, dry Saturday in February, I took my own car out to the scene. Considering where Gary Williams wrecked his car, he appeared to be heading South, away from where the chase began.

According to my odometer Gary was a good ten miles from the Judson Road and I-35 intersection where San Antonio Police got involved in the chase.

According to the reports, the chase proceeded south into the heart of downtown San Antonio before the kids were caught. So, obviously, Gary must have been heading for the Perrein-Beitel and IH-410 interchange where he would hop on the loop, head east, and catch southbound IH-35 and join the chase.

But, that didn't figure either. According to reports, at least five and as many as eight San Antonio Police units closer than Gary Williams responded to the call that led to a one hundred mile chase.

Even if he wanted to make the call he was anywhere from five to seven miles away and he had to go through one of the city's busiest strips on a Wednesday night, just before midnight.

What was Gary thinking? I've ridden with officers who refuse to get into a situation like Gary had leaped into because of the very thing that had happened to Williams. This wasn't revolutionary thinking either. Police officers often get hammered in the press for questionable chases that in some cases end in the loss of innocent life.

Not to mention the fact that cadets and veterans have a very strict chase policy drilled into their heads from the first day in the Police Academy. But, that doesn't keep some overzealous officers from jumping into the fray against better judgment. Williams was looking, more and more, like that kind of officer.

Apparently, the police chief was forgiving in the matter, because I could find no record of disciplinary action taken against Williams for that wreck.

I kept Williams actions in mind and searched on, coming to the reports on the complaint for using excessive force filed against Williams one week before his death. It was deemed unfounded.

Cynthia Orr had found that complaint to be the weakest of the two. In her examination of the records, she had noted Williams had no cover officer.

However, the Internal Affairs investigation included a statement from a cover officer who claimed that he had been present at the incident but did not see Williams strike anyone with a flashlight.

I stopped reading for a moment and tipped my chair back to think. Too many things just didn't add up. First, a cover officer, then no cover officer. Gary Williams flips a patrol car for no apparent reason and doesn't even get reprimanded.

My mind spun with the possibilities. Gradually my thoughts quieted. I decided the spectra of the drug revelation was tainting my insight, because I was beginning to see a conspiracy in everything. That's the time, I thought sighing, to take a deep breath.

I did one better. I called in sick on Monday and took the day off. I call it a mental health day. My daily life was fraught with tension; my case was still in court, the Hernandez brothers were in jail and apparently not going to be tried for quite a while, and the fallout was still heavy nearly a year after the shooting. It all added up to overload.

The work environment wasn't going that well either. Though Ron and I had come to terms on the station's stance and my legal representation, things had changed at KMOL.

Many of the people involved in helping me with the original flurry of Hernandez stories had been sacked during the upheaval. Now, once again, some of the old-hands bailed out and changed jobs.

We had new anchors and new middle-management. Susan Tejeda, who'd done some of the follow-up reporting on the original Hernandez stories was now in Los Angeles, along with her former weekend co-anchor Art Rascon.

Joe Vasquez was in Houston as was Sharon Adams—the former attorney/courthouse reporter and our morning anchor, who'd made fun of me every day for about a year and consequently had many times kept me from taking myself or my situation too seriously.

Dave Roderick, our veteran city hall reporter who couldn't believe that anyone would think that a confession obtained by a reporter could be admissible in court, had left to be a producer in Minneapolis.

New faces filled the newsroom, and although I'd been at KMOL less than two years, I suddenly found myself one of the "old-hands," with the emphasis on *old*.

Chapter 17

A Yo-Yo Existence

I spent my birthday on Saturday, March 10th, 1990, in a blue funk. Macon told me the Criminal Court of Appeals was probably going to hand down a decision in my latest appeal soon—probably on the following Monday. Naturally it wasn't supposed to be in my favor.

I was on the downward spin of the yo-yo again.

"Reporter Facing Fourth Jail Trip," The *San Antonio Express-News* headline said on Tuesday, March 13th.

"This sucks. I'm getting tired of it," I told *Express-News* reporter Richard Smith.

"Brian Karem goes to jail!" Edward T. Shaughnessy, the chief of the appellate section of the Bexar County District Attorney's office reported with glee.

I didn't have the opportunity to respond to that one.

A majority of justices handed down the decision, which did not include a published opinion. They didn't even think enough about my position to offer their opinion. This did not look good.

The district attorney prepared a warrant for my arrest: Jail once again loomed ever larger on my personal horizon, when fate in the form of a federal judge stepped in.

United States District Court Judge H. F. "Hippo" Garcia signed a stay order the following Tuesday, March 20th, so I could once again plead my case—this time in federal court.

"This is one big weight off my shoulders," I told Michelle Salcedo who was interviewing me for her story in the *San Antonio Light* the following Wednesday. "At least I can go to work tomorrow and not worry about going to jail during the middle of a live-shot."

The stay order did not make Pat Priest, the judge in my case, feel any better. The Hernandez trial was scheduled to start on April 23rd, and it now looked like it would be postponed again.

"I'm pretty much resigned to not getting a trial until the fall in that case," he dejectedly told reporters.

The upshot was, once again a scheduled trip to court—sure a different court room, but most of the players would be the same.

"This is our best shot," I heard Macon tell me again, just before the April 5th hearing. "The U.S. Court of Appeals in New Orleans has recognized a privilege for reporters in some cases, so since we fall under that court, Hippo might see things our way."

I love Larry like an older brother, but I don't think even he believed that.

Federal court in San Antonio, where John Woods sat as a judge before Woody Harrleson's (of "CHEERS" fame) father assassinated him, is a huge round building of immense proportions. Its court rooms, in contrast to the county court house just a few blocks away, are huge, stately, and somber. Perhaps the atmosphere inspired some deep thinking, because during our April 5th hearing, we finally got down to what I believed was the heart of the issue—a reporter's right to gather news without being impeded by the state.

Gerry Goldstein and I were crossing swords that day.

"So in terms of the magnitude of the need for any evidence which might assist our clients, you would acknowledge, would you not, that there are few cases in criminal jurisprudence where issues can have greater magnitude than where someone's life lies in the balance. Is that a fair statement?" Gerry asked me.

"That was quite a statement, I'm sorry. I . . . could you state it again?"

He repeated his words.

I took a deep breath and began slowly, earnestly.

"I think there are greater instances. I think that is one of the greatest, yes."

"There are greater?"

"I believe so."

Gerry seemed genuinely surprised. He smiled, "They tell us in law school never to ask this next question," he said. "What would those be?"

"In my opinion?"

"In your opinion what would have a great consequence than the State . . ."

I broke in, "Taking someone's life?"

His voice became more accusing, "Executing you. If you were the person whose life was at stake, what would you place greater value on than your life?"

"Well, you didn't ask me if I was the person. I mean, obviously, I'd have a vested self-interest in that case."

"All right. I didn't ask it that way. That's correct."

"But if you're asking my opinion," I paused and

looked directly into his eyes, "I think anything that would trash the Constitution would have far greater consequences than a single life. I think that would affect all of us in the country . . ."

Silence filled the room for several minutes. Then he countered, "When you described the First Amendment privilege which you are asserting today, you described it as a qualified privilege. Did you understand that when we use the term qualified privilege that, generally speaking, those are privileges which are qualified or must be balanced against other interests in a given situation?"

I believe I surprised him again with my answer.

"I don't believe that balancing my interests versus the defendants' is what's at stake here. Because I always believed that the Constitution was devised not to pit individuals against each other but to protect us from the excesses of government. So maybe the State should have no choice but to drop the charges against your client."

That was the heart of the matter, what I'd been struggling to make everyone understand from the very beginning. In my opinion, the State simply didn't have any right to rely on me to do its work. The world would be better off if this were a working reality, rather than an ideal to strive for.

"I'm not sure my client would disagree with you on that Mr. Karem," Gerry Goldstein said quietly.

With Gerry's questioning now behind me, things, it seemed were going my way. Maybe my yo-yo existence was on an upswing.

Even the Judge seemed genuinely friendly and polite. John Primomo, Hippo Garcia's magistrate, conducted the hearing. Afterward he would write an opinion that Hippo Garcia could either sign off on, or ignore.

Primomo seemed concerned, throughout the proceedings, with who exactly was on my notes, which, of course, was what the fight was all about. He seemed to indicate that if no one else in law enforcement was listed on the notes other than Harlon Copeland and Alex Ramirez, I might have cause to keep my notes and consequently my sources confidential.

A question he posed to me during the hearing seemed to confirm my reasoning.

"And my question, which if you can't answer it, don't answer it: Is there anyone else involved with the State, some other type of state law enforcement officer such as a city police officer or someone else whose name is on that list?"

"I can answer that: no, there isn't."

I felt more at ease in federal court and felt there was a much better chance I'd get a fair hearing there. This, I convinced myself, was the last appearance I'd make in court. The federal magistrate would soon stop this nonsense and I could go back home.

"Don't do anything to anger the magistrate," Macon had said.

"Hey, I won't. I've done all right so far in court, haven't I?"

"Yes. But it's very important we don't mess up now."

Macon wasn't taking any chances. Maybe he really believed this was my best chance. By God, he almost had me believing.

Beth Taylor, of course, tried to throw cold water on my soaring spirits. On this day she decided to be called as a witness, rather than act as a prosecutor. Evidently, she wanted to testify as to my lack of character in the previous court hearings.

On the stand, she claimed that she was called to defend justice, and she said there was every indication I was a pathological liar. According to her, I never once said my notes only contained names and telephone numbers. It appeared that after many months of testimony, she was still convinced that I was hording something she desperately needed to make her case.

At this point Larry dramatically held up two transcripts, one from the May 10th 1989 hearing and one from the February 8th 1990 hearing, he pointed out that indeed all I ever said I had on the notepad were names and phone numbers.

Beth's temper sparked and she went on to defend the State's contention that I was the only source for finding out who'd set up my jailhouse interview with Henry Hernandez. This argument had been used time and again as leverage for prying my notes from me. The State needed it, the argument went, and since I was the only one that had the information, then I had to give it up.

A few minutes later when Mark Stevens began to question Beth, the real fireworks erupted.

"Ms. Taylor, you've been present at all the hearings in which Brian Karem has testified in regard to this case, have you not?" Mark asked.

"Yes."

"Now, you started to answer a minute ago and I'd like to hear your answer about any doubts you may have about Mr. Karem's credibility on particular issues."

Her voice hissed, "In the last . . ."

She never finished. Macon jumped up and cut her off. "Your Honor, for the love . . . excuse me. For the record, I am going to object that I do not believe that's an appropriate question."

"Sustain the objection," Primomo said.

I almost passed out right there. I think it was the first time any judge had sustained any of Macon's objections during the year we'd been involved in this case.

But, Mark Stevens didn't give up. "Well, in your knowledge of Brian Karem over the course of this case, have you had occasion to formulate an opinion about his character for truth and veracity?" he asked Beth Taylor.

"Yes," came her reply.

"What is that opinion?"

Larry was up again. This time he groaned. "Your Honor . . ."

"It's bad," Beth cut in before Primomo could shut her off.

Now Larry was really pissed. "Your honor, for the record I'd like to object to that, that's . . ."

"Sustain the objection," was all Primomo said. I was stunned again. Larry scored twice.

Larry must of liked it too, because he said, "Thank you, Your Honor," as he sat down.

Primomo added, "The answer's stricken from the record."

Now it was Steven's turn. I was a no good, dirty rotten sonovabitch, in his eyes, and he wanted it on the record.

"Your Honor, with all due respect I think it's admissible under the Federal Rules of Evidence. She's had occasion to observe Mr. Karem. She has a basis for her opinion and she stated it. I . . ."

"I have a transcript of the prior hearing, Mr. Stevens. I'll make my own determination about his credibility." Primomo's steel edge voice indicated his judgement was final.

"That's all I have . . ." Stevens sat down and the

assault on my character, at least for the time being, was over.

But, my appearances in court, apparently, were not. Primomo called Macon and I back for a closed door, in-camera, hearing the following day.

In-camera hearings are supposed to be strictly off the record affairs. Oh, everything is recorded, but the notes and transcripts are sealed and not for public consumption.

In other words, the judge wanted to talk off the record with me as I do with my sources. "Okay," I told Macon.

Primomo quickly got to the heart of the matter. He asked me about my sources. He didn't want to know who they were, but he was very interested in what they were, how they participated in the story process, and how I conducted the interview with Henry Hernandez.

Realizing this was my best opportunity for escaping an extended stay in jail, I tried to cooperate as best as I could without compromising my promise to Henry's cousin.

I told Primomo that the guards seemed really reluctant to have Henry Hernandez talk to me and they had broken up our first conversation when Henry had said, "The guard's back and I have to go . . ."

I also told Primomo that my third source never talked to Henry while on the telephone with me.

Primomo wanted to know how the telephone call was made, and I told him I thought Henry had probably made a third party call; since I had been told that after subpoenaing the telephone records no one could find records of Henry calling KMOL. Of course, I didn't tell him that I deduced Henry had called Debra first, and then called me.

A short while later the questions turned to

Debra's relationship with the Hernandez family. I testified that Henry told me his father didn't get along with my third source and there was an ongoing feud in the family. I reported on calling "this person" back and during that conversation "this person" said the same thing. In addition, she said Henry's father hated the person, had made life unbearable before, and if the person's name was ever associated with my interview, then Henry's father would make it hell for the person.

Macon nodded as I spoke. Later he asked if I had any reason to believe that this person had contacted Henry prior to his arrest.

"No," I replied.

"I didn't think that the person (Debra) had any personal knowledge of the crime itself."

The subject turned to KMOL's preliminary investigation and how everyone thought that Williams had actually set up a meeting with the Hernandez brothers in order to purchase drugs, after which something had gone wrong which led to the shooting.

I stressed the fact that my third source knew nothing of any of this.

"So, as far as you know," Primomo inquired, "this person has never actually spoken to Henry David Hernandez about the circumstances of the murder?"

I looked into his eyes. "I'm pretty sure this person hasn't. This person didn't want to have anything to do with it. The less this person had to know about it the better is the feeling I always got."

Primomo excused Larry and me a few minutes later. We drove back to his office and discussed the case.

"How did it go?" I asked tiredly.

"We took our best shot," he said. Not a particularly encouraging comment I thought grimacing.

We changed the topic of conversation and drifted

over to my feelings of unhappiness at KMOL. Forrest Carr was a thorn in my side, and Ron and I weren't getting along the same way we had in the past because of his reluctance to back me because the Holguin tape became public.

Larry leaned towards me, "Listen, Brian, I'm going to be honest with you. You do your job well, better than most. I don't know another reporter in town that could go through everything you've gone through as well as you've gone through it."

"Yeah," I said dejectedly waiting for the other shoe to drop.

"But," he flashed his genuine smile, "you tend to piss people off. You tell them exactly what you think. The only place I know where you can get away with that any more is in the law. You can be an absolute asshole, but if you're a good lawyer, then people have to deal with you. They don't have to deal with you at KMOL. If you're good, but you piss people off, they can just fire you."

"True. But, what are you suggesting, that I take up law?"

We both laughed. I have a whole family filled with lawyers. I'd opted not to go that route many years ago. But, I've had to rethink my opinion of attorneys at least once that I can remember.

It happened while I was covering a trial, an Associated Press reporter who knew my father's brothers (both of which are attorneys, one is a judge and the other a state senator in Kentucky) asked me what my father did for a living.

"He sells cars for a living."

"And your uncles are lawyers?"

"Yes."

"And you're a reporter?"

"Yes."

"Geez. Couldn't anybody in your family find an honest way of making a living?"

On April 10th, Judge Primomo issued his fifteen page recommendation. "This Court concludes that Karem has no right to refuse to disclose the names of his confidential sources," Primomo said.

Primomo quoted a long litany of cases, including Supreme Court decisions which he used to back up his recommendation.

It had no power, since he was only a magistrate. However, Primomo had once been a clerk in Garcia's office before becoming a Federal Magistrate, but the news was not good. "The judge usually rules along his magistrate's recommendation," Macon warned me.

There was a bright note. In the final six pages Primomo issued an alternate recommendation, which Garcia could follow if he wanted to.

"After at least two evidentiary hearings in state court and one in federal court, neither the State nor the defendants have shown any reason to believe that disclosure of the names of the confidential sources is necessary to prove the matters for which their testimony is sought," Primomo wrote.

He also commented favorably on my credibility, which had been a prime target of Stevens and Taylor during the past year.

"Although they contest Karem's veracity, the Court finds his testimony on this matter to be credible."

What gave Larry, Ron, and I the greatest hope, though, was Primomo's conclusion that "There is no compelling need for disclosure (of the source) . . ."

All the law enforcement forces had been exposed, he noted and, "although the State and defendants suggest that Karem's notes contain more than names, addresses, and telephone numbers, the Court finds Karem's denial of this allegation to be credible."

Although the primary recommendation called for me to go to jail, we all clung desperately to the hope that Judge Garcia would choose the alternate recommendation.

Nervously I waited for the judge to rule. Macon said he knew him well enough to try and convince the judge to rule in my favor. But, no one was holding their breath.

The tension rose. Primomo, the nice magistrate had already decided I had no privilege to protect, but if someone above him thought I did, then the prosecution and defense hadn't met the test for making me turn over my sources.

I didn't know whether to smile, cry, or pray. As it turned out, I did a little bit of all three during the next few weeks.

And, as if everything else wasn't bad enough, two other incidents in my life during those weeks showed me I must have parked my wigwam under an especially dark and nasty cloud.

On May 24th, 1990, I found myself covering the state legislature in Austin. Lawmakers were discussing school reform, talk is about all the legislature had managed to do on the problem for about twenty years. But, with the threat of a court taking their law making abilities away from them, legislators were finally moving forward with an education reform package.

During the middle of this stressful session, Senator Carl Parker began blasting his fellow senators for not having the courage to do anything. My photographer and I were standing in the back trying to photograph this mess when the photographer leaned over to me and said he couldn't get the shot because one of the senators, who appeared to be inebriated, was swaying back and forth, in and out of our camera shot.

I leaned over to the senator in question and asked him if he'd please move so we could get our camera shot. He responded by saying, "I'm a Texas senator, Buddy, and I can stand wherever in the FUCK I want!"

His response was so loud it could be heard in the senate gallery and the Lieutenant Governor damn near stopped the debate to find out what had happened.

Naturally, I was kicked out of the senate.

"It's just another part of the legend you're creating, Brian," Richard Smith reassured me even as he wrote the story for his paper. I wasn't too cheery about it.

But, I was less cheery, even down right frightened by what happened to me a short while later.

On the night of June 6th, Pam and I were returning from a relaxing evening at a friends house. We'd spent the previous weeks with friends, searching for some calm in our lives, hoping I wouldn't go to jail, and trying to prepare for that eventuality.

I'd had a couple of drinks that night; so Pam decided to drive our 1987 Firebird home. I had the seat fully reclined and decided to snooze for the fifteen minute ride home.

As we pulled into our subdivision, I heard Pam say, "I think someone's following us."

"Turn into that near by cul-de-sac so I can see." Our pursuer responded by trying to run us off the road. I tried to keep my cool and sat upright. I desperately wanted to take the wheel, but there was no way to switch drivers.

Instead, I told Pam to drive back down the main road to a convenience store where a cop could often be found. It was about a mile away, but it was our best bet.

Pam drove like a professional racecar driver, weaving around one car, running a red light and pulling up to the convenience store. Our pursuers were right behind us.

As the car skidded to a stop, I hopped out. Luckily, there was a cop parked outside of the Stop-N-Go. I started waving and hollering.

"This guy behind me is following us and trying to run us off the road!"

As I said that, the car, which I could now see was a Ford Mustang, sped past me, hung a left against the light and headed eastbound. The cop jumped into his car and took off after him. I got back in our car.

"What do I do now?" Pam asked.

"Follow them."

We took off. At the next intersection at least four kids bailed out of the Mustang, which continued to roll down an incline toward a grocery store. The cop had probably called for back up, but at the moment he was outnumbered.

I yelled, "Pam stop!" and then bailed out myself.

Knocking on the window I called out, "Lock the door. If anybody comes, take off."

I ran toward the closest kid I could see; a fat boy who was running behind a gas station. I made for him.

Rounding a corner in pursuit I damn near collided with a drunken guy wearing pointed-toe boots.

"Hey what's happening?" The guy sputtered.

"Some guys tried to run me off the road!" I screamed back continuing my pursuit.

"Great!" he said, joining the chase. "I love a fight."

A few seconds later I caught up with the boy and

put my football training to use as I hit him with a tackle and knocked him to the ground, head first.

Then, I rolled him over and put him in a choke hold.

Suddenly the guy, who'd decided to join me, began kicking the kid all over. He grabbed the kid from me, stood him up and began to hit him in the mouth, the stomach, and the kidneys.

I ran to get the cops, thinking my new found partner was going to kill this kid, and I still didn't know what was going on.

The cops had turned the corner, but my partner and the fat kid were gone.

We had two boys though, both about fifteen years old, one white, one black.

The cops ordered the tall white boy to stand near the police patrol car.

"What are you doing?" the older graying cop asked him.

"I was just along for the ride."

"What were you doing?" he pressed.

"They didn't see the dude, man. They didn't see the dude."

"What were you doing?" The older cop's face reddened. He was now controlling a growing rage. The kid knew it and buckled.

"They were gonna do her, man. Then take the car."

"Do her?"

"Yeah, rape her."

I flipped. Every bit of frustration with KMOL, jail, gangs, the Hernandez brothers, Gary Williams, came pouring out.

I struck the kid as hard as I could. The force of the blow resounded through the night. He flipped over the police car.

The cops quickly grabbed me and pushed me against my car. After lecturing me on what I did wrong and how I might now be arrested, one of them commented, "Well, that might well be the only punishment these kids get," he said, frowning.

"What were they doing?"

"Well, they stole that car at gun point from a seventy year-old man about thirty minutes ago. They threatened to shoot the guy in the head with a 9mm; then they smacked him around and stole the car. It looks like you guys may have been next."

Six cops had arrived at the scene by this time and while I know at least the first two had seen me hit the kid, they let me go and told me to go home. I was lucky.

"Do you think this has anything to do with the Hernandez brothers?" Pam asked me when I got back to the car.

"I don't know. I don't know. Let's go home." She was in tears. I was too.

Afterward I thought the incident was probably just some bizarre coincidence which drove home the violent nature of San Antonio Streets.

The following Monday I found out the fifteen year old boy I had chased down and tackled had a gun. Police picked him up on the following Wednesday.

Through that experience, I began to understand why some cops on the street are afraid. At fifteen, few kids think of dying. Most males are exploring their sexuality, their machismo, and looking for trouble. They're hooked on the excitement of the experience not the consequences.

That night I also began to understand why cops get upset. We ask them to catch criminals; then if they're juveniles, we want them to babysit 'the kids' and put them back on the streets hours later. Or, if they're adults, the cops catch them and the overcrowded prison system spits them right back out on the streets.

I understand why some cops get stressed out and end up at the end of their ropes, deciding to extract their own justice. I understand why they would turn to drugs or end up shooting someone who might be an innocent civilian.

Make no mistake, I do not condone it, nor for that matter do I condone what I did that night. But, as a human being, I understand vigilante justice on a level I'd never contemplated before the night some fifteen-year-old with a 9mm decided to take a joy ride and rape my wife.

Chapter 18

Six Months in the Hole

The road was long and winding, as the song goes, but since it had led me three times to jail, the journey was not one bit enjoyable. By the spring of 1990, I was getting so desperate to avoid another incarceration I decided to take the unprecedented step of trying to contact the judge on the case.

Dear Judge Priest:

I'm taking this rather unique step of writing you to see if I can get you to reconsider the order of contempt you've issued against me.

I'll be brief. The information so desired by the prosecution and the defense is readily available and I believe both sides may already be in possession of that information.

I've talked with Alex Ramirez. He was the main source for the story. I approached him with my desire to speak with Henry Hernandez and it was Alex who took my hand-written message with the telephone number on it. He came forward of his own free will. He says that he has been interviewed as have at least two other members of the Sheriff's Department concerning this case. His statement has been taken. He is clearly a member of the law enforcement community. Yet, we've not heard in court what he or the others he names can tell us about the case.

It is not my intent to stand in the way of justice, but is it not possible that the defense and the prosecution could talk with those who have firsthand information and possibly know more about the telephone call that was made—other than me?

I have a 15-month old son and a wife, both of whom I love dearly, and I do not enjoy the fact that I may leave them for six months. I constantly ask myself if justice is served by jailing me. Obviously, I think not.

I believe your decision sends a chilling message to journalists. I believe the Criminal Court of Appeals sends even a colder message to reporters. I see a time in the not too distant future when the media has become so weakened by First Amendment erosion that all of us are going to be forced to live with journalistic pablum like "Entertainment Tonight." Let's face it, that kind of reporting is easy. It is neither challenging for the reporter nor for the audience. It is exactly what we get when we tell reporters that journalistic enterprise, integrity and hustle will be met with a court date and harassment—without cause.

> *There's very little good reporting going on now. Please do not help it all evaporate.*
>
> *Thomas Jefferson once said that he had "sworn upon the altar of God eternal hostility against every form of tyranny over the mind of man."*
>
> *I do not pretend to have the intestinal fortitude nor the brilliance of Jefferson. God knows he would probably face my situation with more courage than I am. But, I do. It isn't right. The press does a lot of things wrong, but we are venturing in dangerous waters when we make reporters little more than tools of the state. I ask you to reconsider your decision and, at least, have the defense and prosecution explore every angle before I'm asked to divulge my sources.*
>
> *Thank you,*
>
>
> *Brian J. Karem*

Pat Priest's office returned it without his even taking a look. His secretary told me the judge didn't want to prejudice an ongoing case by reading a letter from a witness.

I should've figured.

By the end of June, 1990, things were really looking grim. Unfortunately, my wife's company had scheduled a business trip for her. Although she tried to get out of it, she couldn't. She left June 21st and was expected back by June 27th.

During the interim, Federal Judge Garcia ruled against KMOL's appeal, and I was once again facing the prospect of having a warrant issued against me. Moreover, I heard Mark Stevens was working overtime to acquire the document in order to toss me in jail a fourth time.

On Monday, June 25th, 1990, I dropped Zack off at the day care center next door to the station. I got into work around 8:30 A.M. Saying good morning to the staff, I sat down at my desk.

The telephone rang almost immediately. A very good law enforcement friend of mine was on the other end of the line.

"Get out of the newsroom and disappear!"

"Why, is there a hit out on me?"

"Yeah. In a manner of speaking. There's a sheriff's deputy on his way over to arrest you. The court issued a warrant today and you're going to take a six-month sabbatical at the Harlon Hilton if you don't get out of there."

"Thanks, I'll make tracks!"

I hung up, relayed the information to Ron and quickly headed out the door. A few minutes later a deputy appeared at the front desk looking for me, but I was already gone.

I stopped by the day care, picked up my son, and spent the rest of the afternoon at home watching *The Jungle Book* with Zachary. Zachary thought getting to spend the day with his dad was great, but I was shaking with fear. I didn't answer the phone or doorbell.

Topping off my worries was the fear I'd get arrested before I could find someone to watch Zachary. Calling my Dad, I explained my predicament. It eased my mind when he promised to come over as soon as he got off work.

Next, I called my wife and told her the bad news. We shared a brief moment of anguish—she couldn't get home any sooner than Wednesday morning and it looked like I might not get to give her a hug or a kiss for about six months.

Following that depressing revelation we both hung up and I placed a telephone call to Larry Macon. He promised to file an immediate appeal with the Federal Fifth Circuit Court of Appeals in New Orleans.

"I expect I can get to work on that appeal tomorrow," he told me. "If I fail there, the only recourse left is to appeal to the U.S. Supreme Court."

"Jesus."

Now I felt really desperate, but Larry calmed me down.

"We've known it could go this way for a while. I'll do everything I can. You just concentrate on taking care of your family."

"Yeah. Thanks Larry."

"You scared?"

"To death."

"Well, hang in there. Don't call anyone else; don't do anything. Stay at home and just stay quiet."

"All right."

"Have you been able to contact Henry's cousin Debra at all?"

"No. As a matter of fact, since the family told me she moved out of town, I have no idea where she is."

"If you have any magic cards up your sleeve, now would be the time to pull them out."

"Yeah. Yeah. Don't know what they could be, but I'll think."

"Okay. Call me later."

I hung up the telephone and slowly walked back to the living room just in time to see Kaa the snake try and hypnotize Sherekhan the Tiger in one of the closing scenes of *The Jungle Book*.

"Oh no, I can't be bothered with that. I have no

time for that sort of nonsense," the Tiger said as he slapped the snake to the ground.

You see the Tiger was on his way to eat poor old Mowgli the man cub, and couldn't take the time to indulge the lowly snake.

At that moment a funny thought crossed my mind. Larry Macon was Kaa. Pat Priest, Mark Stevens, Beth Taylor and Gerry Goldstein were Sherekhan. I was cast as Mowgli.

That depressed me so much that Zachary and I took a break from the movie to eat some ice cream.

In the kitchen as I ladled the chocolate scoops into sugar cones, it hit me. If anyone knew how to contact Debra, it was Henry Hernandez. Since I'd gone to the wall for Alex Ramirez, maybe I could get him to put me in touch with Henry one more time.

I called Alex. He wasn't around, but Tom Barry, the jail administrator was.

I swallowed hard. Technically, I was a fugitive from the law. The sheriff's department had a warrant for my arrest and was searching for me. I, in turn, was calling the sheriff's department chief jailer to have him put me in touch with another prisoner.

My plans could easily have backfired, but I was too desperate to care. Luck was with me. It worked.

Once again I was put in touch with Henry Hernandez.

"Henry, I've protected Debra for a year and a half, man. Do you think she'll let me tell her name now?"

Henry was characteristically quiet, stoic almost. "Yes. I think so. Thank you for your help. I think it's" he stuttered over the next few words, "okay that you tell her name."

"Henry, I really need to hear that from her. Is there anyway I can get hold of her?"

"You . . . you can call my sister. She can get in touch with her and she'll help you."

"How do I know that?"

"Tell her that we talked and I told her to help you."

He gave me the telephone number and his sister's name. I thanked him and asked him how he was holding up in jail. He said it was okay, but he missed his family. I thanked him again, wished him luck, and hung up the telephone.

His sister, unfortunately, was not very sympathetic.

"You called my brothers animals," she said. "Why should we help you out at all?"

I winced. That stupid telephone call to Jimmy Holguin was coming back to bite me in the butt once again. I quietly cursed myself for having made that damn telephone call.

I tried cajoling. I tried sweetness. I tried begging. She wasn't budging. She refused to help me contact Debra, although Henry's sister let it slip that her cousin was once again in town.

That was a ray of light in an otherwise extremely, dark tunnel. I called Macon back and let him know.

Before the day was over I'd talked to Jeanne Jakle, Kym Fox and many other reporters as well as an investigator who was attempting to find Henry's cousin. At eight o'clock that night, I gave Zachary his bath. My dad came over shortly thereafter with our friends Rochelle and Joe. We put Zack to bed and I spent the rest of the evening playing word games and trying to keep my mind off the threat of incarceration. I had two last hopes: Larry's appeal to the 5th Circuit in New Orleans, and the investigator I'd called who was attempting to get hold of Debra Ledesma.

In bed I tossed and turned unable to sleep. With

Pam out of town, and the warrant hanging over my head, my nerves were frayed to the breaking point.

Tuesday morning brought word that the Appeal to the Fifth Circuit had failed. At noon the investigator called to say he couldn't find Debra. By then I was in a panic.

Late Tuesday afternoon, Macon informed me he'd forwarded an Appeal to the United States Supreme Court.

"Larry," I said unable to keep the agony from my voice, "I can't keep this up forever. Something's got to happen."

He sighed heavily.

"The pressure's may build more. You know that."

I didn't see how it could get much worse, but he was probably right. I decided I'd turn myself in to the authorities the following day. I wanted to wait until Pam got home, but it looked like that wasn't going to be possible.

I called my father and made arrangements for him to watch Zachary and feed the dogs and cats.

Then, I called Ron and let him know my plans.

He said KMOL would contact the rest of the local media.

Tuesday, I spend another sleepless night.

Wednesday morning, I tiredly climbed out of bed, fixed Zack and I some breakfast, got us both dressed, and drove him to day care. As I bent over to kiss him goodbye, I suddenly realized it might be six months before I could do that again. I clasped him to me one more time. Then I went to work to face the music.

My Dad met me at the station at nine. KMOL-TV called a news conference announcing the time when I would turn myself into the Sheriff. Then we called the Sheriff and gave him the details.

Afterward I taped an interview for a spot that would air later that night, after I was in jail. It felt a little like giving the eulogy at my own funeral.

I spent some time talking with Ron, Forrest, Bob Donahue; the gloom was apparent. One bright spot came when Dan Lauck, for whom I have unqualified respect, came over, shook my hand, and told me I was doing the right thing.

Then the station brass hopped into a couple of cars with Dad and me, and we drove downtown. I was scared and nervous.

Arriving at the jail accompanied by my father, Bob Donohue, Larry Macon, and Ron Harig, I saw members of the press lining the steps shouting questions. It looked very intimidating.

It's one thing to spend your adult life in front of a camera covering the news. It's quite another to be there making it. But there's no way a journalist can be hypocritical. Everyday he has to intrude into other people's lives. When it happens to him, he's got to take it.

Two of my best sources inside the sheriff's department, both undercover policemen, walked me to the front door where I met the sheriff and discussed my jailing with the reporters who gathered around us.

"I sure don't want to do six months in jail, but as I think I've told all of you, I made a promise and I think you know what that promise entails, and I intend to keep my promise," I said.

"I'm not going to give up my notes. I sure don't want to spend six months in jail, but there aren't many times when you get to live up to your principles. This is one of those times."

Six Months in the Hole

A young woman reporter, her rimless glasses perched precariously on the tip of her nose, called out to the sheriff, "Will he get special treatment in jail?"

"All my inmates get special treatment," Copeland said. "They have a good bed. They have color TV, and they get fed three times a day."

Smiling, a blond, suntanned thirtyish man asked Bob Donohue, KMOL's station manager, if I were going to be paid while I was in jail.

"Of course," he said.

I'd never thought otherwise, but it was nice to have it on the record.

After the brief press conference, I was led to the bowels of the Bexar County slammer.

Tom Barry gave me two choices. I could stay in a lockdown cell for twenty-three hours a day and come out one hour a day for exercise, or I could go down in low risk and stay there with twenty-three other inmates who were in for minor misdemeanors. In Bexar County that means traffic ticket offenders and dead beat dads who don't pay their child support.

"If you don't think it's going to be too bad, I'd recommend the low risk," Barry told me. I nodded agreeably. The thought of being tied down to a 5×7 cell for twenty-three hours was too claustrophobic for me, and I figured I could handle myself with the tame bunch in low risk.

I'll say this much for jail. You learn quite a few lessons there.

You lose all sense of self-worth and all sense of independence. Nothing is more symbolic of this than the fact that you must give up your own underwear. Giving up a good clean pair of laundered shorts in exchange for a pair of dull gray boxer shorts that have been worn by thousands of people of questionable hygiene before you, and have the stains to prove it. After that, nothing of your identity remains. You go in as you came out of the womb; there's nothing more frightening than going to jail.

"I did the Lindbergh kidnapping and I was behind the grassy knoll when Kennedy was shot," I told the jailer who handed me the shorts. "I figure if I start confessing now, then maybe I could keep my own shorts."

He wasn't amused.

As I waited to be told what to do next I suddenly realized this was it. No more reprieves. I'd done everything I could to protect my sources and stay out of jail. I'd failed. Now it was up to Larry Macon and Ron Harig.

Before being taken to my cell I made a phone call, which all inmates are allowed to do. Reaching KMOL I found out that Ron was going on vacation starting the following Monday. I was stunned. How could the news director take off on me while I was in the Bexar County jail? Not only was he deserting me, but Forrest Carr, the very same Forrest Carr who'd inspired such low levels of confidence from Larry and me when we'd met previously, was going to be left in charge and would be my contact to KMOL.

"Larry, this doesn't look good." I told him when he came to visit me that afternoon.

Larry, now had the greatest responsibility resting squarely on his shoulders. He was left as the last, best hope of saving my carcass.

Larry is one of the hardest working attorneys I've ever met. He's entirely dedicated to his job, oftentimes, his secretaries told me, spending night after night in his office working.

But the pressure was beginning to show. He looked noticeably worn and frazzled, and practically jumped on my words.

"I'm not for it myself. But, what can we do?"

Not much, we both soon found out when Larry's appeal to the Supreme Court failed.

Justice Byron White didn't see things our way and turned down our request for a stay of my jail sentence pending the outcome of our final appeal.

Larry told me the news, grim faced. But, he also told me not to worry, he was going "shopping" for a Supreme Court Justice more sympathetic to the First Amendment.

With my history this search didn't look promising; it was looking more and more like I'd spend the next six months in jail.

"I hated to be the bearer of bad news," Macon told me when we discussed the matter during one of his subsequent visits. "But, if the prosecution and defense feels strongly enough about this matter, they can ask you to serve another six months in jail after you finish this term."

"What?"

He shrugged, a trifle sheepishly, "That's right. Theoretically, as long as you refuse to turn over your notes, they can go after you."

With a flash of emotion, I asked, "What?"

"Of course, that probably won't happen."

"Probably?"

I was flabbergasted. What was I going to do? Serve a life-term for keeping my mouth shut?

"Look Brian," he said patiently then added, "that's the worse case scenario. Let's just concentrate on getting you out of here right now."

Chapter 19

Buzzard's Luck . . .

Life in the low risk area of Bexar County jail is fairly routine. I lived in a V-shaped dormitory with twenty-three other men who'd been locked up for a variety of mostly silly reasons.

Between the two legs of the V-formation of bunks which lined the walls, there lies the bathroom/shower facilities. These are easily monitored by the one unarmed guard who is on duty in the "pod." This guarantees that no inmate can do something the guard isn't able to see. Of course, this means absolutely no privacy either.

If you've never had to go to the bathroom with two dozen people watching, believe me it's a humbling experience—especially if your guard is a woman. And, on one eight-hour shift, it was. She was a nice, stern, older black woman, and though I respected her and even liked her, I couldn't pee or crap in front of her. Consequently, I became quite adept at holding my bladder and bowels for marathon lengths of time. At the time, I couldn't believe that newly developed ability would be able to serve me outside of the jail, but I was proved wrong.

I was told, by several, this habit I developed made

me a "character" since I was too embarrassed to urinate or defecate in front of a woman. There were more than a few guys in low-risk who found that activity to be fun and I knew one guy (that *I* considered to be a "character") who tried to time his bladder release so he could urinate as often as possible while a member of the opposite sex was on duty and could watch him.

There were a variety of characters in low-risk, but none turned out to be a greater friend and a greater character than forty-four-year-old Clifton Hurd.

Hurd, who slept in the bunk next to mine, passed his time playing solitaire, for which he proclaimed he had buzzards luck since he rarely won. He also walked around the cell, shuffling his rubber slippers against the floor with his hands stuffed inside the front of his loosely fitting orange jail pants, and all the while puffing on a hand-rolled cigarette and shouting in a Jamaican accent about his need to introduce massive quantities of any legal or illegal drugs into this system.

"I want some cocaine!" he'd shout. "I want some dope! I want to get high!" He was, perhaps, the sanest man in my cell.

People left Hurd alone, and with good cause. He told me he was in jail for "slapping the taste" out of his sister's mouth. When he found out I had a little trouble with a judge he offered to take care of it for me for a mere $50. For that price, I was told, a friend of Hurd's would pay a little visit to Judge Pat Priest, concentrating on his kneecaps.

I politely turned down the offer.

Another one of the characters I met in the jail was a young man whose name I never learned. He roamed around the pod moaning that he'd never drink "Thunderbird" again in his life.

I had to ask, "Why?"

"Because whenever I do I get arrested," he said.

As it turned out, he got drunk on Thunderbird, went inside his house, got his dad's gun and then came out and shot up the flower pots.

"Nice," I said.

"Yeah, what a bummer," he said, and then he began picking at his toenails.

All in all though, life in low-risk was fairly dull. Although there were some dangerous felons in my pod, most of them were in this time for misdemeanor traffic offenses. They weren't about to sacrifice the easy living in low-risk by making things violent. They knew they'd end up on the tougher upper floors of the Bexar County Jail where the pods were so overcrowded that three people were sometimes forced to share the same 5×7 cell.

I was about the only person in the pod that ever had visitors. Karen Conley, a state representative tried to visit me. Bexar County Judge Tom Vickers paid his respects as did most of my friends from KMOL. Those visits helped keep my spirits up and meant a lot.

Some of the visits didn't work out well, though. In particular, visits with my father were horrible. Angry at my incarceration he couldn't control his emotions. He turned purple and blustered that he would waste the judge, Beth Taylor, Mark Stevens, and most local members of the bar association.

Pam was having a very difficult time because she had to handle my father's emotionalism, and also because of problems she had been having with other local members of the media. She became wary of trusting anyone. Even some of our friends were looking for a quote.

Some of the reporters who hassled Pam wanted to know if I was going to jail to try and boost my career. Obviously, they had never been separated by three inches of glass and kept from embracing their loved ones. But, Pam stayed committed to me in spite of all this. She was my anchor and without her I could not have made it.

By the second week, I'd settled in. I had begun a journal, played Spades more than I'd ever wanted to, or even dreamed I'd wanted to, and beat a couple of selfprofessed chess experts at their own game.

Each day breakfast came very early, around 5:30. Then we spent the morning cleaning our day room and our bunk areas. By 10:30 we had lunch. In the afternoon we were free to watch television, read, or even go outside our pod for an hour of recreation in the gym. We had dinner by 4:30 P.M. and then we had the late afternoon free to watch more television, read, play cards, or whatever until lights-out came just after the 10 P.M. news.

The guards made one concession to me on the television viewing. They usually watched KENS news in the low-risk pod, but upon my arrival the guards let us watch KMOL. This allowed me to keep up with news about myself, as the station did at least one story a day on my incarceration.

Each day my picture ran, with a little title like "Day 10."

Inside the jail all the media attention became a double-edged sword of unbelievable proportions. I had to be careful not to flaunt the media attention, lest I incur the wrath of some inmate—like "Baby Huey" —who thought I was being mollycoddled.

Baby Huey, as he was called, was a big, fat, ugly white guy. I don't know what his real name was. He began bitching to the guards that I was getting away with murder inside the jail and that I was a favorite of the jailers. When no one was looking, he'd shove a broom or a mop at me while we were doing our daily cleanup chores in an effort to trip me up, make me fall down, smack me, and generally humiliate me.

One thing I learned quickly was that you couldn't allow anyone to bully you. It would only get worse.

So, I had to pick my time. One day, when the guard wasn't looking, Baby Huey tried once again to knock my feet out from underneath me with a mop. I turned quickly, with broom in hand, and stuck him hard in the ribs with the broom handle. He slipped on the wet floor and fell next to the toilet. The guard heard the commotion, jumped up and ran over to us.

"What happened?"

"He slipped," I said.

"Yeah, I slipped," Baby Huey said. After that he gave me no more trouble and he was rotated out of the pod two days later.

Chapter 20

Sodomy No!

Twice during my incarceration I ran into Henry Hernandez. Both times I was heading to a visit.

Henry's appearance shocked me. His face was pale and drawn. The legirons and shackles he dragged along weighted down his thin body and made him appear incredibly frail.

The first time we passed each other I said, "Hi." A flash of recognition spread across his face and he smiled, then waved. The second time we waved at each other and passed without words.

Meanwhile, the second conversation I had with Henry immediately prior to my incarceration was succeeding in ticking off Mark Stevens. He once again claimed the call I placed to find out how to get hold of Debra was a blatant violation of Henry's civil rights.

"I'm flabbergasted. I was shocked when I heard this," Stevens told local reporters.

Stevens concluded the second telephone call was an aberration of jail policy. Sheriff Copeland and a Captain in charge of the jail at the time denied any knowledge of the call.

* * *

I also ran into several guards who'd been with the Hernandez brothers during their first days in jail. It all helped to bring greater depths to the personal side of a tragedy that was affecting my life, Henry's and the Williams' family.

On June 28th, Justice Byron White sent a simple letter to Larry Macon concerning my request for a stay of my jail sentence pending the outcome of my appeal:

"The application is denied."

Larry gave it to me when he visited me in jail a few days later. He was looking terrible and I could tell he was working his ass off trying to get me out.

Wednesday, July 3rd, Larry wrote to Justice William J. Brennan Jr. in an effort to find someone on the Supreme Court who would at least listen to us. Brennan was the only justice who said he'd give our case a reading.

"This is a matter of utmost constitutional importance," Larry wrote to Brennan. "Brian Karem, a journalist, is incarcerated under exercise of his constitutional right to protect a confidential source. The appeal before the Fifth Circuit is proceeding. In the interim, we ask that you issue a stay, as Mr. Karem has no relief available to him but for action of the Supreme Court."

Less than a week later Larry got the news. In what was one of Brennan's last decisions, he put the case before the entire Supreme Court for a vote. Some saw it as a test vote on the case itself. Others did not. But, by a 7-2 vote, with Brennan and Marshall in the minority, the Supreme Court voted me down.

Things never looked more bleak.

Then, in walked Forrest Carr. With Ron Harig gone on vacation for a week, Forrest who had seemed so uncaring about my predicament had now decided to take my cause on as a one man crusade. He wrote letters to the editors of both papers, called the networks about the story and generally bullied and pushed his way into making the national media pay attention to our story.

"These guys are jumping up and down on the Constitution with hobnail boots, and somebody ought to kick them in the pants," Carr said of Pat Priest and everyone else involved in the case.

I was floored. Larry was stunned.

I found myself calling him two or three times a day and inevitably he had several reporters lined up for me to talk to. Once it was a drive-time talk show in Denver. Another time an interview with Japanese reporters. I even did a Russian radio talk show. That was my personal favorite. The Russians seemed dumbfounded by the fact that they could talk to me while I was in the slammer. They also spent a good deal of time asking me how much I made for a living and discussing the differences of lifestyles in our two countries.

Forrest got us on *Night Line, CNN Cross-Fire,* and while shake ups in the Soviet Union usually dominated *NBC Nightly News,* KMOL and the First Amendment case found itself as the lead national story one night on *Nightly.*

On the Fourth of July, Faith Daniels read the lead-in to a story that described my case as one "focusing on the rights of American journalists."

Forrest, of course, couldn't have been happier about the exposure.

"First and foremost, we hope the national attention will get Brian out of jail," Forrest told Jeanne Jakle, although he acknowledged the chances of that were slim.

Still, he plodded on.

He even wrote to President George Bush:

> "... I am not exaggerating when I say that journalists all over the world are watching to see what happens to Karem. Freedom of the press and freedom of speech are the two basic rights that make all other freedoms possible. At a time when other countries are making great strides in the field of human rights, now is not the time for the United States to send a message that we're no longer interested in freedom ..."

Forrest says the president never acknowledged receipt of the letter.

But, that didn't slow Forrest down. He also wrote an open letter to the district attorney, defense attorneys and everyone else connected with the Hernandez case.

He beat up hard on Beth Taylor, accusing her of trying to use me as a scapegoat in a case she knew she couldn't win. He accused Mark Stevens of using me as a scapegoat to delay the trial for as long as possible in order to get an acquittal. Since Henry Hernandez obviously knew who helped me set up the telephone conversation, Forrest figured that Stevens knew as well.

He called for everyone to drop the charade, and for the Judge to release me.

It didn't work, but it sure got a lot of press play and the more he spoke, the more people began to listen to what Larry and I had been saying for a year and a half.

Forrest's energy inspired us. Still Larry and I were tired and sore.

Sore, or not, we had one more hurdle to overcome.

Local reporters organized a jail rally in my behalf which was scheduled to take place Thursday, July 5th.

More than one hundred local journalists showed up for this media event.

I was even allowed to witness it. The sergeant took me up to the seventh floor so I could look out a window and down onto the throng of reporters below. Somebody had a pair of binoculars and we all got a pretty good view of things.

Many of the participants carried signs that said "Free Brian Karem." I even saw my son Zack with one that said "Free My Daddy." Some of the signs, like the large blank one my old friend Bud Humphrey brought, were symbolic of what the press would soon be like without the protection of the First Amendment.

One of the signs caught a sergeant's attention.

"Karem, what the hell are you telling people about what goes on in here?"

"Huh?"

"Look." He handed me the binoculars and pointed at a petite gray-haired lady who was milling about the crowd. I trained the binoculars on her and tried to read her placard.

"Sodomy No!" it said.

"Holy shit!" I said.

"Yeah, what's the meaning of that?" the sergeant asked again.

"How the hell would I know, I've never seen her before in my life! Honest."

Mike Martin, the assistant jail administrator, began laughing. "She comes to all the jail rallies and always carries that sign, no matter what the event."

"Great," I said.

A few minutes later the main anchors from all three television stations took to the microphones and began speaking. I couldn't hear the conversation of course, but from where I sat, it looked animated.

Then, County Judge Tom Vickers stepped up to the microphones. Later I found out he'd related an experience I'd had with him about six months previously when his house burned down.

Though Vickers was usually well dressed, hair never out of place, I saw him the night his house burned, sitting outside, in his pajamas with his head in his hands. He didn't even have on a pair of shoes. This bothered me because of nails, glass, scorched wood, twisted metal, and everything else left over from the fire, so I reached into the back of my car and pulled out a spare pair of tennis shoes and offered them to him.

Well, Tom evidently remembered that act of kindness.

Then, the crowd started to disperse and Sheriff Harlon Copeland walked up to the microphone.

I couldn't hear what happened next. But, people stopped leaving. Carey Cardwell, an editor from the *San Antonio Light* walked up to the microphone as Harlon walked away. Carey said something and all the cameras began following the sheriff.

"I wonder what the sheriff had to say?" I mused.

"I don't know what it was, but it sure got everyone's attention," Mike Martin said.

"That's for sure. I wonder what the hell he said?"

I found out moments later when I got back to my cell and called the station.

Harlon Copeland's comments were electrifying. He said he was tired of everyone accusing him of being my third source. He was tired of the political football that was being played. He knew who the third source was, and it wasn't any jail employee.

"The third source is Debra Ledesma, and she's a cousin of Henry Hernandez," Copeland told the world.

As he stepped away from the microphones, Carey Cardwell was the first to regain his composure and said, "I'm sure the sheriff will be available for additional questioning if needed."

I was stunned. Not that someone had found out who my third source was, but that the sheriff had broadcast the news.

"I'm surprised," Larry Macon told me when we talked later. "Here the sheriff is with that bumpkin image and he found out what the police, the district attorney, and the defense couldn't find out."

"More than likely he was the only one who wanted to find out," I told Larry.

"How do you think he found out?"

"Wouldn't be that hard. Maybe Henry or Julian told him. Maybe he checked the telephone records, who knows?" I really didn't care how it was out, just that it had finally happened. Now I thought I'd stand a pretty good chance of getting out of jail.

Larry went to Judge Priest's chambers and asked for my release from jail. But, the judge wouldn't budge. He wanted me to disclose my source in a public courtroom.

I was now in a real pickle. The sheriff had named the right name, but I hadn't talked to Debra yet to see if I could go public. The judge said I had to.

"The judge can go to hell," I told the *San Antonio Light* reporter who called to interview me. "He wants me to come in on hands and knees and give up my source in front of the public. I won't be intimidated."

"You're still full of piss and vinegar, Karem," Larry quipped when he visited me the following day. "Ron won't be too happy with that comment."

I shrugged, "Well Larry, what have I got to lose. It's not like Pat Priest can do anything else to me. Shit, I'm already in jail."

Larry gave a subdued laugh, "Still, he might release you soon. Mark Stevens knows how to get hold of Debra Ledesma . . ."

"There's a shocker, huh."

"Right. But I don't think anyone's going to interview her until Monday. You're going to be stuck in here for the weekend again."

"Larry, hasn't anyone brought up the fact that since Mark knows how to contact this woman, that his entire persecution of me has been a sham? I think he knew all along who she was and what role she played in this, and he never did anything but keep his mouth shut and go after me."

"You think the Judge would have noted that?"

"Yeah. He's only stalling for time, trying to keep his case out of court as long as possible."

Of course, this was old territory for both of us. As early as the April hearing in Judge Primomo's court I had voiced an almost identical concern.

It mattered little. I spent another weekend in jail.

Finally, on July 9th, the attorneys set up a long distance telephone call deposition with Debra in California. Apparently she'd only been back in San Antonio for a few days and then left once again.

On Monday, July 9th, Stevens and the rest of the attorneys succeeded in getting a telephone deposition of Debra Ledesma-Salama.

"Debra, this is Mark Stevens. You and I have talked on a number of occasions, have we not?"

"Yes we have," Debra said establishing the tone of the deposition.

Debra went on to tell of her participation in the telephone call I'd had with Henry. She claimed she never knew she was the "third source" everyone had been looking for, although her participation in the telephone call had been well established in open court on a number of occasions. She also said she didn't ask for confidentiality, or say that she was afraid to come forward. But, then she contradicted herself later.

"I was going to say, ask a question also. I would like, really prefer, if they wouldn't bother me at work because it's very important for me to keep my job, and I really enjoy what I do. So, if possible, is there anyway that I could have no one go there?"

"Does anyone have a problem with that?" Mark asked the assembled attorneys.

"Because I do not want them to release my married name or where I work or where I live," Debra cut in.

The news that she wasn't claiming me wasn't a big surprise. Since the Holguin interview had become public, certain members of the Hernandez family had distanced themselves from me. I was sure this was more of the same.

On the subject of the telephone call, Debra testified that she was at her mother's house for a party on Easter Sunday 1989. She knew nothing of Henry's involvement in the murder, she said, until the media reported it.

She said she was at home with her aunt the night of March 28th when Henry called home.

"There was a number to dial. Okay. And at that time, I thought it was for a friend of his. So, what I did, I dialed the number and I put the phone down to give him, you know, give him privacy because I thought it was for a friend. I didn't know what I was getting myself into actually. Okay?" Debra said.

According to Debra, Henry told her to stay on the telephone, and then in Spanish, said, "estos vatos estan poniedo presion." That means, "These people here are putting pressure on me." But she didn't know what he was referring to.

About half way into my conversation with Henry, Debra said she became curious as to what was going on. Henry had already asked her to, so she picked up the open receiver. According to her, I had no idea she was there. That part she got right.

"He wasn't aware that someone else was at the line, on the line. He didn't know that I was on the line, because I remember Henry said, 'stay on the phone,' okay. So I stayed on the phone and I was just listening to the conversation. And after that I interrupted. Because he had asked him two questions at one time and Henry does stutter. . . .

"I interrupted when I said, 'have you investigated on police brutality? Is there any background on that? Is there anyway you could find out?' And right away Mr. Karem said, 'Who is this? Who's on the other line?' "

"Did you ask him to keep your name a secret?" Mark asked.

"No, I never did. I can't remember if he might have said he volunteered that . . ."

"I've never know this man, and I've never really heard of him, because I've always listened to a channel 12 station actually."

A sharp slap. Nobody remembers the third rated station. Oh well.

Despite her assurances that I'd volunteered to protect her name, and she never requested it, she again asked for protection from the attorneys. "The only thing is my employment . . . my job is very valuable to me . . . I don't want no news media around me. Nothing, whatever, nothing to do with that."

Curiously enough, those were very nearly the exact words she'd used with me in our earlier conversation. I believed her then and I believe her now. I had no problem making the promise of confidentiality to her, and despite what she later said, I'd do it again.

She placed the length of my conversation with Henry around forty-five minutes, or at least thirty to forty-five minutes and said she heard beeps during our conversation "that means you're being recorded. It's only common sense. Anybody would know that."

Of course, there were no beeps.

But, she did testify that Henry gave me permission to record the interview.

In addition, she said she was going through personal problems at the time and had given me a telephone number to call her after the newscast.

"Like I said, me and my husband were together at one time, but we separated and we were going through personal problems with our marriage . . ."

When asked if she heard anything on the telephone that led her to believe that Henry had been coerced into making the telephone call, she said she heard voices like they wanted Henry to get off the telephone real quick.

When asked if there was any fear about releasing her name now, she again said:

"I don't want people calling me at work."

"But you have no fear that . . ." Mark Stevens started.

"I have no fear."

". . . That your name will threaten your job in any way?" Mark finished.

"It won't threaten my job. The only thing is I don't want nobody going around my job," Debra answered.

She testified she was nosy about the shooting after it happened, didn't know I wore glasses (referring to the pictures that ran of me in most newspapers in the country on the day I was taken into custody), or was married or had a child. Further, she said she had talked to me that night, after the shooting, but didn't know if she had ever talked with me again.

"I believe so. I don't remember if he had called again to try to get me again to verify that person. I really don't remember. You see, it happened so long ago, you know. He could have tried to call me again and, I don't know. He could have talked to my sister too and asked for me. I think he had called one time and my sister told him I wasn't there. Because my sister and I look alike a lot and we have actually the same voice."

A short time later the deposition ended with Debra once again asking that she not be contacted at work.

That night when Larry visited me at jail, he gave me his grim conclusion.

"She sold you out," he told me.

I sighed heavily, "I can't live with it. I don't like it, but I can live with it as long as I get out of here."

Then Larry asked me the question that I had so often asked myself, the one which would haunt me for many months to come.

"Was it all worth it?"

I still had no answer ready.

I'd been jailed four times for not revealing my source. Alex Ramirez, although later recounting it, had once denied being a source. Debra denied it, although both obviously were. Neither had come forward until pressured or their cover had been blown, yet desperately both had also denied at some point in time that they wanted confidentiality.

KMOL had paid probably $100,000 in court costs. I was locked up, watching my father suffer, and unable to see my son but twice.

My family life was in chaos. My wife was trying to deal with my father's emotional upheaval, caring for Zachary, going to work, fending off a carnivorous press, and trying to squeeze in daily visits with me.

The Holguin interview had been used against me, and there were now sharks circling, trying to destroy my credibility and thus my ability to perform my job adequately.

I knew all the negatives. Yet suddenly, it was all so clear, "Yeah, it was worth it," I told Larry quietly, firmly." I made a promise to someone, and I kept it. End of story."

The day after Debra Ledesma testified I got up early. Larry came to visit and told me I had to appear in court. Dressed in my orange jail togs I was hauled over to the courthouse and herded into one of the holding cells on the ground floor of the Bexar County Justice Center.

Moments later I was notified that I was going back to the Bexar County Adult Detention Center, because Judge Pat Priest didn't want me appearing in court in a jail uniform.

So, I was handcuffed, put in the back of a paddywagon, and driven back to jail. There I put on a suit my dad had dropped off at the sheriff's department for just such an emergency, then I was once again handcuffed and driven back to the justice center.

After about an hour of waiting in the depths of the courthouse in an icy holding cell, I was marched up to Pat Priest's courtroom.

The court was called into session. Then I was paraded out into the courtroom and took a seat on the witness stand.

"Daddy! Daddy! That's my daddy!" I turned to see Zachary and Pam sitting in the front row of the court room along with my father. Pam was smiling, my dad's eyes were red rimmed, and Zachary was pointing at me. I smiled and waved.

I wanted to cry.

Instead, I turned to face the judge. He asked me, in light of the new testimony in the last day, if I had any objection to turning over my notebook.

I am an extremely stubborn man. I still didn't want them to have MY NOTES. But the prosecution and the Defense now had all the information I had protected.

I had made my point, protected my source, and stood up for the first amendment. I could see no reason to continue fighting. The battle was over; so I let them have my one page of notes.

The judge shook his head and told me I could go.

I was taken back into his office.

"When can I go home, Larry?" I asked looking at Macon.

"I think it will take a couple of hours to get everything together. You should be free this afternoon."

But, Larry was wrong. The Judge's order took effect immediately. One of the bailiffs came back and told me the Sheriff's department was already getting my stuff together. My locker would be cleaned out and all my belongings would be waiting in the Sheriff's office upon my return.

I turned to Larry and thanked him.

"Next time, just burn the damn notebook," he said turning to go.

I walked out of the courtroom and met a tearful Pam holding Zachary by the hand. We all embraced, not wanting to let each other go. I looked around and saw my dad walk up crying. I gave him a hug too.

"What's the first thing you're going to do Brian?" one of the crowd of reporters asked me.

"I'm going to have a cold beer and a pizza." I laughed. (The next day, when that comment hit the newspapers, I had about a dozen offers for free food and beer from local restaurants.)

After that I answered a few more questions; then Pam and I walked downstairs carrying a sleeping Zachary.

On the way out of the courthouse, someone handed me a bumper sticker that read "Free Brian Karem." It was a nice little souvenir.

Chapter 21

Now What?

Immediately after leaving the courthouse, Bob Donohue, Ron Harig, Larry Macon, my father, Pam, Zachary, and I stopped at the "Cadillac Bar" for my first real meal.

For the rest of the week, I took it easy, stayed at home, played with Zachary, and got reacquainted with Pam.

Then, the following Monday I went back to work.

One of my first orders of business was to talk to Ron Harig. I was hurt and a little angry that he'd left town while I was going through hell. I thought he'd abandoned me and I was sure it was the Holguin tape and our earlier arguments that had caused him to do it.

Ron said he tried everything he could to keep from going on vacation, but it was prearranged and he couldn't reschedule. I gave him the benefit of the doubt.

It took a while to get used to being back on the job and back on my beat. The summer had exploded in violence as San Antonio's emerging street gangs tried to gain control of their individual corners of the city.

During this period drive-by shootings, long a staple of violence in San Antonio, increased nearly tenfold.

We were on our way to a record year, as most of the rest of the nation was, in murders and every other category of violent crime. Most of this violence confined itself to crimes of passion and gang warfare, but there were notable exceptions. On August 2nd Saddam Hussein invaded Kuwait. All five bases in and around the San Antonio area went on alert and prepared for Operation Desert Shield and the Desert Storm.

My court problems hadn't ended either; I was in constant contact with Larry Macon and Beth Taylor. Larry kept me sane and focused, while Beth nearly forced my heart to stop: she became nice to me. She informed me that since my legal debacle was now in the past, she was going to call me as a witness for the prosecution.

"I want no surprises on the stand," she told me with a half smile.

"Fine, ask me anything you want. Not that you haven't asked me enough already," I told her in a meeting at her office.

"Do you think Henry killed Gary Williams in self-defense?"

"If you're asking me do I think he should have killed Gary Williams, no. If you're asked if I think he killed him in self-defense, I'm not sure. But, if you're asking me if *he* thinks he killed Gary Williams in self defense then I'd have to say, yes. I talked to Henry not too long after the shooting and I think he practically relived the shooting when he told me about it, and I think there's no doubt in his mind that he had to kill Gary Williams."

"That's all that matters," said Jamie Boyd, the newly appointed first-assistant to Fred Rodriguez.

"I just don't want any surprises," Beth repeated, and this time she wasn't smiling.

My future court appearance as a witness concerned me deeply. I was also concerned as I had been since the ordeal began, about a Texas Shield Law. I'd talked with a few legislators who said they'd sponsored such legislation. I even gave a copy of some existing Shield laws to different legislators, but so far nothing had come to fruition. I kept on trying.

Meanwhile, Hollywood sharks had been calling me since I'd been released from jail. My appearances on *Nightline, Cross Fire* and numerous radio talk shows across the country had stirred up interest in the First Amendment. Some people even telephoned me at KMOL claiming to be Hollywood producers who had produced several "Movies of the Week." Each said they were interested in my story.

Pam and I discussed the situation and concluded that if everyone who claimed to have produced a "Movie of the Week" had actually done so, then people had been producing a "Movie of the Week" back to about the fall of the Roman Empire.

Time passed, my personal life got back to normal. Crimes usurped media interest. One day in the early fall I realized a year and a half had gone by since Gary Williams had been gunned down. A year and a half and the two Hernandez brothers still hadn't gone to trial. Their latest November trial date had now been postponed to the following January.

That gave me some time to try and dig up additional information on Williams.

I still had a lot of unanswered questions. A prominent one was what about this rumored ring of drug dealing cops? Frank Castillon and I had talked several times. He said he had his suspicions, but he hadn't found anything out. I talked with a local lawyer in town who'd also heard the rumors—supposedly from a cop. The name of the gang was "The Rebs" and they were supposed to work out of, primarily, the northside substation.

I tried to see if anyone had heard of this group, but as late as October of 1990 I had no luck.

Then, there was Sue Carter—Gary Williams girlfriend. I got hold of a police investigative report that showed that four months after Gary's death the police had searched her home as well as Gary's wife's home. At Sue's home they found syringes with residue inside, but no identifiable illicit drugs.

"Jesus. Four months after the fact they search this home," I told Greg Trimble when we talked about the matter. "What the hell does that tell you about the scope of the police investigation?"

"Doesn't look like much of an investigation, brother."

"No shit."

I was also curious about the statement Chief Bill Gibson made about Gary's habits prior to his death. He was described as a loner, supposedly because he was so much older than the other officers. The chief and the department blew that off, but I was curious as to whether or not that was supposed to raise a red flag. If an officer did, in fact, act like that, was someone supposed to notice or do something about it, or did they routinely let that kind of behavior go on? The ramifications were pretty astounding to me—especially considering that another loner by the name of Stephen Smith had turned into a one-man judge/jury/execution team.

When I contacted former Chief of Police Chuck Rodriguez, he said that type of behavior was extremely atypical, and had he been in charge, he would've acted differently.

"Cops aren't loners," he told me. "And when one of them starts acting like he is, then there's definitely something wrong. His sergeant should've noticed it and done something about it. And if his sergeant didn't do anything about it, other patrolmen should've mentioned it to someone. He needed counseling."

Rodriguez's testimony might be discounted because he'd been canned following the Steven Smith scandal, which he'd failed to notice or act on, but on the other hand, who would know better than Rodriguez about lone wolves on the department.

I talked with police brass that I trusted and they backed up what Rodriguez had told me.

Meanwhile, Sue Carter was refusing to return my calls.

On the other hand, Cynthia Orr, Gerald Goldstein, and Greg Trimble were still talking with me, and Beth Taylor was still after me to be a witness in the trial: so I wasn't completely shut out.

One of the biggest mysteries that Greg and I came across was something Gary Williams supposedly said while fighting with Julian and Henry.

"You can go home now. You can go home now," is what Gary supposedly said while fighting with the two. Henry had mentioned this to me in passing and Greg said Henry was emphatic about the proclamation.

Greg though, was stumped. Why would the officer say that while fighting with the two brothers?

I thought I finally came across the answer when talking with Goldstein. What if, after being shot, Williams told the two Hernandez brothers to take off.

That might make more sense. If Williams thought he would live, that is. My idea was that Williams knew he was stoned and he didn't want anyone around. It was just an idea though. There was no proof, just questions, and to me, some plausible answers.

There was also another riddle to be unraveled. How stoned was Gary Williams when he died? We heard all kinds of speculation from addicts, cops, and doctors who told me what the usual dosage might be for everyone from a first-time speedballer to a veteran addict. But, I hadn't heard anything that could pinpoint exactly what amount Gary had ingested into his system.

Through a friend, I obtained the Brook Army Medical Center reports and the Emergency Medical Service reports.

The reports also showed other things of interest. One notation showed that Gary Williams had at least twenty units of blood pumped through him. Another notation mentioned fifty units. Despite all that blood that was flushed through Williams' system, he tested positive for drugs after his death. He even had it in his bone marrow, which, Dr. DiMaio explained, eliminated the possibility that the drugs were in the transfused blood.

The hospital notes also included a number of operations performed on Williams. I talked with a doctor who said this was inconsistent with a patient who was close to death. You only do what you have to in order to keep such a patient alive, he said. When the patient is stable, that's when you do the other, nonessential surgery.

I took all of this information to Ron and suggested we do a story. He thought about it a minute and then suggested that I continue to gather information, and when the moment was right, and we had a good hook, we could do it.

So, I went about my daily routine, covering the escalating crime rate, shenanigans in the state house, and other news on my beat. On the side, and on my own time, I continued to gather information about the Gary Williams' shooting.

And the more information I gathered, the more I became convinced that the Hernandez brothers were being wrongfully held in jail. I was also convinced the district attorney was determined to keep the Hernandez brothers there, even though Julian's involvement seemed minimal and Henry may very well have been fighting for his life at the time.

Chapter 22

Who Hustled This Whole Deal?

In late November of 1990 I was sent to the Persian Gulf for a week to cover the local deployment of troops in Operation Desert Shield. Not long after I returned, Bush decided to launch the air war against Baghdad and the Hernandez case once again blew up in the San Antonio papers and on television.

On January 15, 1991, as bombs fell over Iraq's capital Henry David Hernandez spoke for the first time in court.

Mark Stevens put him on the stand "for the purpose of vindicating our Fifth, Sixth, and Fourteenth Amendment rights," he said.

In Henry's quiet and civil manner he testified that it was Alex Ramirez who first came to him in jail and suggested that he talk to reporter Brian Karem. According to him, Alex had said Julian told him to call the reporter. Henry also said Alex encouraged the call, "So you could get your story out."

"It would be to your benefit if you called this number and talked to this person, so all of us could know your side of the story," is what Henry claimed Alex told him.

Henry said, "Well you know, my attorney had advised me not to. And he (Alex)—well he said something to me I don't remember the exact words, but he said, like you know, 'Well, nobody's going to know unless you call and talk to this person here.'"

Then, since Henry's cell didn't have a telephone in it, Alex moved him to a cell that did.

After I called Alex to find out why Henry hadn't called on time, Henry said Alex came back and rushed him saying, "Come on, call that number!" Henry said, "I already did. He's just getting on the phone. And he walked up to me and grabbed at the phone and he said, 'Who is this?' And I guess Mr. Karem said, 'well, I'm Karem,' and he said, 'Well okay.'"

Beth Taylor tore into Henry's story. She brought up his previous aggravated assault charge which had been dismissed and another pending murder charge.

Then, she went after the statement that Alex had engineered the interview for his benefit.

"Did you voluntarily, say the words you said to Brian Karem, did someone force you to say those words to him?"

"In a way I was pressured into saying that in more ways than one. For one, Alex Ramirez pressured me into going to a phone and calling. And then again, I was pressured by Mr. Reid as he kept coming over and saying, 'Come on, call this, call that number.' Plus I hadn't slept all night, you know, so I wasn't thinking straight."

"Did they force you to say the words you said?" Beth was relentless.

"No, but I wasn't in my right state of mind and I didn't know exactly what I was saying."

"Did anybody put a gun to your head to force you to talk to Brian Karem?"

"Okay, no. No."

Then, as Henry continued, he said he felt railroaded and then said he talked to me about maybe five or ten minutes.

He said he didn't remember calling me back a second time; he just remembers calling once.

Then Beth hit him again:

"Did Brian Karem force you to tell him whatever you said?"

"Not physically, no."

"Did he force you or threaten you in any way?"

"No, he didn't."

Well, at least there was that. It wasn't a glowing endorsement, but at least Henry hadn't answered yes.

Beth again began pressing Henry. She hoped to show that Henry had told several family members the exact same story he told me, and by consequence, it had been his intention to get this story out to the public, not some police detective or jailer.

"At that time did you want to get your story out?" she bluntly asked him.

"In a way I did, but not the way that it came out."

"Why not the way it came out?"

"Because they didn't put it out right. They made me sound like I was saying something else, which I wasn't. I was saying something different. He left out too many things from what I said and what he censored it to be said."

I sighed thinking everyone's a critic. But, at least he admitted that he wanted his story out.

Then, after saying the deputies put him up to calling me, he went on that "they came in and told me, 'Hey, come on hurry up, hurry up,'" insinuating that Henry should get off the telephone.

"Did you want to talk to the press?" Beth asked him.

"Maybe I did, but I never told anyone I did."

To be perfectly candid he never told me he did, but plenty of other people, including his own father, had indicated as much.

The testimony continued for quite a while, while I was present in court. Then Mark Stevens asked that Pat Priest "invoke the rule" which meant witnesses present in the courtroom had to leave until they had to testify.

I sat with Alex, Greg Trimble, Joe Hernandez, and other witnesses in a small room just next to the courtroom. I thought it was silly to invoke the rule on me. I'd testified to the same thing literally a half of a dozen times since May of 1989. Did Mark actually think I was going to chance my testimony now?

Whatever, I had to listen to Henry by putting my ear up to the door to the room in which I was kept. I left the door slightly ajar to facilitate this process, despite the protests of the bailiffs.

What were they going to do? Throw me in jail?

After lunch, I was once again called to the stand. It was getting to be a habit.

Once again Mark Stevens went after me. He again tried to show that I'd concocted things with the full cooperation and at the encouragement of the sheriff's department, the police department, or perhaps someone else inside law enforcement.

At least one police officer had asked me the same thing. Homicide detective Rusty Brown and I discussed the case in the police department's parking lot as recently as June of 1990. He thought that someone inside the district attorney's office was my third source and coconspirator.

He and Stevens obviously had similar ideas. Stevens once again brought up my conversation with Jimmy Holguin and said my conversation was circumstantial evidence that I'd been working with the police the whole time.

He recalled my saying to Jimmy Holguin, "I want to help, brother, tell me anything else I can do."

Damning evidence that I'd begged to help the police and thoroughly brown-nosed Jimmy Holguin. Unless, of course, you consider the fact that the police recorded and provided the tape to the district attorney's office.

I couldn't believe they were still harping on that story that the D.A.'s office had somehow enticed me into interviewing Henry Hernandez. It was true, they would then be involved in its discovery in an open courtroom. In fact, the only reason that Beth Taylor would want to make my taped conversation with Jimmy Holguin public, was if she firmly believed I had additional, unedited raw tapes hidden under my desk.

She had certainly argued that way in court. It was a gamble on her part, and one in which she bet the wrong way. If she got me to break in court and admit there were other raw tapes being horded at KMOL under my desk, she could later use this to destroy my credibility if Mark Stevens wanted to argue that the very same taped conversation showed the depth of cooperation between me and Jimmy Holguin.

"He already admitted he lied once in this courtroom," Beth Taylor would then be able to say in court, "How can anything he say be believed?"

Fortunately such a scenario did not play out. I didn't have any missing tapes to turn over, no matter how much the D.A. argued to the contrary.

So, now Mark Stevens could use the audiotape with impunity.

Yet, common sense would also show how ludicrous this all was. If the D.A. had very little reason to make the tape public, then the police department had absolutely no reason to give the tape to the district attorney—if indeed I was working hand-in-hand with Jimmy Holguin. He'd be the world's biggest fool if he not only recorded a tape, but helped to make public a tape that showed him in collusion with a reporter.

Still Mark continued pushing.

"Hey look," I finally said from the stand. "If I was in bed with the prosecutors . . ."

I had to stop. Beth had a very nasty look on her face and even the judge snickered.

"No. Really, if I was in bed with the prosecutors as you would have everyone believe, then why would I do a story that said there were problems with the police officers?"

"A lot of things don't make sense, Mr. Karem," Mark answered.

I breathed in, "Yeah, your whole argument doesn't make any sense."

Stevens did not stop there. He again argued that Henry Hernandez had been forced into talking to me —almost dragged against his will and shoved in front of a telephone and physically manipulated to dial Debra Ledesma and myself.

Taylor argued that if Henry was so scared of being pressured, "Why didn't he have Debra call his attorney? After all," Taylor said, "he'd just gotten done talking with his attorney."

It seemed almost funny to me. Beth Taylor, in what would be her last appearance for the State in the Hernandez case, was forced to argue my side of the case.

She now needed to prove to Judge Priest that I had not been involved in some grand conspiracy with the police department to get a confession from Henry and Julian Hernandez.

"Who hustled this whole deal?" she asked loudly. "Brian Karem did! No one else did any initiation. No one in law enforcement recruited Brian Karem . . . Brian Karem was acting as a nosy, aggressive, pushy, selfcentered reporter who cares only about the case and nothing else matters to him."

I couldn't suppress my grin as she continued.

"He was just doing his job as he sees it, being a reporter . . . Brian Karem being an agent of the State is quite frankly—laughable."

Beth went on:

"All that is present is the manipulation of the system by Brian Karem for the story . . . and quite frankly Brian Karem isn't about to work for the State. The court saw his demeanor on the stand. His contempt. His scorn for the police department and the sheriff's office . . . The State did not use Brian Karem. Brian Karem used the State."

I thought about asking Beth for a letter of reference, but that was probably going a bit far.

In the end Pat Priest, whose kneecaps I'd so nobly defended the previous July, decided he didn't buy Mark Steven's argument. He ruled there was no evidence of collusion of the depth that Mark Steven's tried so vainly to convince everyone.

But, the Judge did say the depth of State involvement was too extensive anyway. In other words, he didn't believe Alex should have passed the note to Henry Hernandez the day I obtained an exclusive interview.

So, Priest ruled the interview inadmissible. The State appealed, and the case was buried at the Fourth Court of Appeals.

After the court hearing, I cornered Pat Priest as

he left his courtroom. I told him I had considered protesting his decision to "invoke the rule."

"I was going to get Larry down here, but I decided against it," I explained.

"Well, I'm glad of that," he said. "It's not that I'm afraid of his lawyering. I just don't like the sonuvabitch."

I nodded. The Judge was still as fond of Larry as I imagined Larry was of him.

Not too long after the January hearing, some of the cast of characters in the Williams' case again changed.

The unthinkable occurred in South Texas. Fred Rodriguez lost his bid for reelection. A Republican, Steve Hilbig, became the district attorney.

Although there was lots of grumbling, many secretly looked forward to Steve's tenure in office. Republican Sheriff Harlon Copeland also looked forward to a member of the same party holding down a high county office.

As a consequence of the democratic defeat, Sam Ponder and Beth Taylor left office and took other jobs, probably with more security and better pay.

That left complete strangers at the helm of the district attorney's prosecution of the Hernandez brothers. At first I thought this was good. Maybe somebody could talk reason to the new guys. I didn't want to testify, and maybe the district attorney could proceed without my help—or drop the charges against one or both brothers.

This did not happen.

In February I had to stop working on the Hernandez story. I'd managed to secure a visa during my previous trip to Saudi Arabia. Now, I managed to secure a trip with another reporter back to the area to cover Operation Desert Storm.

I'd been in-country less than twenty-four hours when someone shouted at me, "Brian! Brian Karem!"

The first thought that flashed through my mind was that someone was serving me with another subpoena. But, when I turned around it was only Kerrie Triplett, a friend of mine from college. He'd seen the news about me on *Nightline* and the national news services and just wanted to say, hi.

Then, I ran into Dan Rather. I introduced myself to him. He knew me from my ordeal and from the letter I'd written to him concerning the shield law. Because of the war, he hadn't responded, but he thought it important.

I got similar responses from other network reporters, and I was feeling pretty good about myself until I ran into a military press officer at the Joint Information Bureau by the name of Colonel Larry Iceonegle.

I wanted the good colonel to take a moment of his time to help me arrange an interview outside of the Dhahran International Hotel with some Texas soldiers.

"I don't have time for you," he told me. "You're a little dog. I have to deal with the network people. They're big dogs. I only deal with the big dogs."

What a come down. So much for notoriety. With the good Colonel I was about as important as a gnat that hangs around the dick of a hound dog.

But, my Hernandez ordeal did prepare me for the Persian Gulf in ways I never thought about. Gabe Caggiano (the reporter who traveled with me) shot for me and I shot for him. We worked with a singlemindedness I didn't think possible for more than a month, around the clock.

And nothing that we went through could shake our resolve to get the job done.

At one point we found ourselves sitting in a hotel in Kuwait City the day after it was liberated. Tom Brokaw sat on a small couch in a room with no heat and little light, writing his part of the *Nightly News*. There was a blood stained sheet on the bed behind him and some of the network guys were busy trying to burn some beans on a hot plate that had earlier burst into flames.

Tim Ehrlinger, a producer for the *Today* show had killed the flames, and then we'd all taken to the food and some bottled water we'd brought with us.

"Ugh! How can we eat this shit?" one of the reporters asked. He was munching at one of the military's M.R.E.s (Meals Ready to Eat is the official military explanation. Many, however, call them Meals Rejected by Everyone).

"Easy, baby. I've eaten Bexar County Jail food. I can eat anything." He looked at me like I was a martian and I walked out to look from our fifth floor window at the bombed out remains of Kuwait City.

It looked eery in the dark. Not a light on. No heat. The oil fires burned in the background like some reminder of the Apocalypse.

I hadn't talked to my wife in days. I hadn't seen her or Zachary in close to a month. I was 9,000 miles away and if something happened to me, she wouldn't know until days later. I could still hear gunfire from somewhere in the city.

I'd just driven eight hours up a bombed-out road where a CBS reporter had disappeared just weeks before. I'd seen mortar fire, interviewed Egyptians, avoided one Iraqi soldier who tried to wave us down on the side of the road with his AK-47 assault rifle in hand, and had negotiated a big Toyota land cruiser through the remains of the battle that had freed Kuwait.

During the preceding two weeks Gabe and I had run probably a hundred Saudi checkpoints. We felt the concussion from the bombs dropped by B-52s. I'd seen dozens of scorched corpses and at one point had to hold my bowels for four days while I sat struck in a convey pounded by an intense sandstorm. (I'd already perfected the practice of holding my bowels in jail.)

I was scared, standing on the balcony looking out over what appeared to be a ghost of a once vibrant city.

But it was okay. It was bad, but not even the Persian Gulf War was worse than the private war I'd waged in Bexar County during the preceding two years.

When I got back to San Antonio, I once again tried to pick up the Gary Williams' investigation. By now the leads were stale. I couldn't see how anyone was ever going to prosecute the Hernandez brothers. Hell, without my testimony, I don't think there was anything at the scene that could prove that Henry had ever been there.

The prosecutor's best witness, the security guard who'd phoned in the call, hadn't been located. The other witnesses contradicted themselves and no one had seen much of the altercation.

What a charade. When was it going to stop? No time soon, I learned.

I walked into Pat Priest's office to find out about the trial in April of 1991. I found a reporter there from the *Express News* talking to a secretary in the outer office.

I asked about the Hernandez case.

"I hope I never have to do anything on that case again," came the answer.

"Isn't it kind of upsetting that they haven't been out of jail in more than two years?"

"No. They're hoods. It keeps them out of trouble if you ask me. We let one guy out for the Fourth of July and he ended up dead. He got shot that night."

That was the prevailing attitude. The Hernandez brothers were Hispanic hoods. Even if Henry had killed Gary Williams in self-defense, he deserved to be in jail.

Chapter 23

Imprisonment Without Trial

Someone bet me that by June of 1991 the Hernandez brothers would be going to trial. I took the bet. Even I can recognize a sure thing when I see it. When the date arrived Judge Pat Priest's secretaries didn't even want to talk about the case. It was the annoying little murder case that wouldn't go away.

"It's all your fault," Mark Stevens needled me. "Without all the press, we'd have this case to trial already."

"Hey," I answered in the same vein, "I'm not the one stalling. You ought to talk to the district attorney and tell them to get the lead out. They're the ones stalling. Your clients should already be free."

Mark had a hard time arguing with that, so instead he took a different tactic.

"Well, why don't you talk to the district attorney about it."

I did. Steve Hilbig was no more informative about the Hernandez case than the last district attorney Fred Rodriguez had been. In fact, he may have been much worse. Fred, at least, made vague references to law when he told me the State had to delay the trial. Hilbig blamed it all on me. It was an argument I had heard before, countless times. It still didn't hold water.

"Steve, it's now been two and a half years since the crime. You've never lowered the bond, downgraded the charges against these guys, let alone drop them. How the hell can you blame me for that?"

Hilbig laughed it off. "Can't take a joke, can you?"

I didn't see what was so damn funny. Hilbig avoided answering the questions I asked and no one in the district attorney's office would even talk to me about the Hernandez case since Beth Taylor had left.

I found myself longing for Beth Taylor to come back. She'd been a worthy foe, and at the very least, she was a straight shooter. I also longed for the State to get on with its appeal of Judge Priest's ruling. Unfortunately, voicing my desires did little to set the wheels of justice spinning. More time went by. The Hernandez brothers stayed in jail and no date was set for their trial. In fact, for 350 days, absolutely nothing happened on the Henry Hernandez case—with a few exceptions. Several dates were set for oral arguments in the State's appeal of Priest's decision. All of them were delayed. The Hernandez trial was once again shelved.

Then on January 9th, 1992, Mark Stevens and a new assistant district attorney met in the Fourth Court of Appeals in the new Bexar County Justice Center to once again argue about whether or not the confession I'd obtained from Henry could be used as evidence against him.

Before the proceedings began, I approached the

bench and asked the assembled justices if KMOL could bring a camera into the courtroom.

Both Stevens and the assistant district attorney strongly objected.

"There's already been enough media attention given to this case," the district attorney argued.

"That's the whole reason why we're here is because of television's intrusion," Stevens added.

The head of the panel was about to rule when I again asked to address the justices.

"Excuse me, but I'm not asking any more than to have the same courtesies that are extended to the print media. They can bring their pads and pencils into this proceedings. The camera is the equivalent of my pad and pencil as a television reporter. Unless this proceeding is to be closed to the public, I would respectfully request that I be allowed the same privileges as my colleagues in print."

The head of the panel, a kindly faced older woman dressed in a black robe said that she had no problem with my request but decided that because both attorneys involved in the case had objected, I'd best sit down and forget that silly notion. It certainly wasn't a complete putdown, but the result was the same. No cameras allowed.

I sat down without further comment. But, I did turn to Mark Stevens and asked him what he thought.

"How'd I do, Counselor?"

"For your first appearance as a lawyer, I'd say not bad." He couldn't suppress the slight smile that played at the corners of his mouth.

"Of course you still won."

"Of course," he said broadly grinning.

It was then I reached the conclusion that I couldn't help but like Mark Stevens.

The court hearing was without major incident or

logic either. Pat Priest ruled that in his court, the taped confession I'd obtained was not admissible in court.

The primary reason for this was the fact that it was not a complete recording. After the editing process, only a few minutes remained. Under Texas law, that in itself made the entire thing inadmissible.

This further explained Beth Taylor's activities when it came to the Holguin tape. She undoubtedly thought she could shame me in open court into admitting I had secreted a "whole and complete" recording beneath my desk and had not given it to anyone.

She had, of course, been wrong, but that damn tape had come back to haunt me so many times, I began to think Taylor must have gotten pleasure out of that fact by itself.

The new assistant district attorney, a petite, blond-haired woman without Beth Taylor's fire nor her grasp of the law, tried to argue, without citing precedence, that the State should be able to use my testimony in their case.

She conceded that the taped confession was no good (since it wasn't a "whole and complete") recording, but she said she still wanted to use my testimony in the case.

The justices seemed stymied by the convoluted logic, as was I and Mark Stevens—who argued strongly against such a measure.

The justices asked a few pointed questions, then adjourned and promised a decision on the tape soon. Soon turned into months. A trial could not continue without the decision and some of the attorneys began to comment that the trial would be postponed until 1993 or even later.

"That's ridiculous," I told Cynthia Orr one evening as we sat discussing the case in her office.

"Well, you're dealing with my docket, Gerry Goldstein's docket, Mark Steven's and the district attorney's docket."

"No, I mean it's ridiculous that these two guys are in jail for years without a resolution. In fact, it's ridiculous that they're in jail at all."

"I agree with that. If this had been two white kids, they'd be out on the street right now," Cynthia frowned at me.

And of course, that was my opinion too. My own experience in jail showed me that very few white people spend any time in jail at all. That's a fact. It was also a fact that Julian and Henry weren't going to get any breaks because of their criminal past and their heritage. Things like that aren't supposed to matter. But they do.

My increasing anger because of the Hernandez brothers continued incarceration led me to once again meticulously go over my notes and files.

Eventually this led me to obtain a copy of the medical reports from the night Gary was admitted to the hospital. The EMS files and the hospital files showed many routine treatments and medications. But the one thing that sounded alarms in my head were the notations that indicated that Gary Williams had more than forty units of blood pumped through his body as the doctors worked to save his life.

The implications of his drug use multiplied tenfold with that startling revelation.

"He had to be ripped to the tits," a doctor told me in the starkest terms available.

"There's really no telling how much of the drugs were in his system, but he had to be extremely high to register anything in his bone marrow and his blood stream after the number of units of blood he had pumped through him."

This information was either unknown or disregarded by the new district attorney, Steve Hilbig. He still wouldn't budge on the matter of dropping the charges or freeing the Hernandez brothers.

"It's because they're Hispanic, isn't it, Steve?" I asked him one day.

He scoffed, "Don't be ridiculous. We prosecute all offenders equally."

Of course, that has never been the case. Some ex-prosecutors and police officers told me they had good information that the district attorney and some members of the police department were determined to keep the Hernandez brothers in jail as long as possible —whatever way possible.

They'd killed a cop, and even if it was in self-defense, even if the cop was stoned to the gills, I was told, the Hernandez brothers would pay nonetheless.

Trying to appeal Pat Priest's decision to exclude the confession I obtained from Henry was the tool to keep the Hernandez brothers in jail the prosecutors could use best.

This sickened me. I had no desire to be used by law enforcement again, especially in this manner.

I took my information back to Ron Harig, along with other information I'd accumulated on the Williams/Hernandez story. I felt it was time for a story update—time to break some new ground.

Ron disagreed.

"Save it," he told me. "Wait until the right time, and then we'll do the story. We need a hook."

"The hook is the recent Hernandez hearing in the fourth court of appeals," I argued. Ron disagreed. I didn't continue the fight. I told him I'd keep digging.

I knew Ron didn't want to go back over old ground. I didn't either. But, there was more to be told on the Hernandez story. I wanted to be the one to tell it.

Meanwhile, we both continued our fight for a Texas Shield Law. I worked with the Media United for a Shield Law group in Houston and Dallas. This entailed talking to reporters who wanted protection from being hauled into court and having to give up sources.

I also did a lot of work on my own, calling reporters, editors and legislators, in hopes of getting some action.

Henry Cuellar, a friend of mine from the days when I worked in Laredo, and a state representative, even introduced legislation in the house based on several shield laws I'd given him.

While that went on, Ron was supposed to contact newsroom managers across the state and get them to help us pass a shield law, or if they didn't agree with a shield law, at least we hoped they'd look the other way.

It didn't work.

Cuellar withdrew the legislation we'd worked hard on after running into a hornet's nest of protest from newsroom managers across the state.

"Look, if your own people won't get on board, how can we make this work?" he asked me.

"It won't work. You're right." I said discouragedly.

So, once again my attempts to help other reporters met dead ends. And while this went on, two print reporters from Houston and one from Corpus Christi experienced nearly the same injustice I suffered as they tried to protect sources for stories they'd done.

"What the legislature gives us today they could take away tomorrow," one newspaper editor told me when he said he could not support a shield law.

"Let them give it to us today and we'll fight like hell to make sure they won't take it away tomorrow," I told him. But my arguments fell on deaf ears.

I continued to speak at colleges and high schools as I tried to convince the general population and other reporters and editors of the need for a shield law.

Everyone wanted to know about my time in jail.

Often I got the question, "Would you do it all again?"

I told them I would, but went on to explain. No issue is as clear-cut as it appears on the surface. "Reporter withholds a source and the television station he works for backs him up all the way to the Supreme Court," is not how it went.

It wasn't that simple.

Ron never really wanted to "go to the wall" as he said, over the case. Because of this I almost hired outside counsel and left the station. In addition, I made a big blunder trying to "shmooze" Jimmy Holguin and the station never came to grips, I felt, with the importance of protecting one's sources and also protecting freedom of the press.

Then of course, everyone I'd shielded at one point or another either denied being a source or denied asking me for protection. This might seem discouraging, and in fact, at times was so to me, but I stressed it didn't diminish the importance of the concept. Neither did the fact that during all this, I had to go to jail four times, nor that my wife and family lived a fishbowl existence where no private life was possible.

I was praised and ridiculed. Loved and hated. Defended and denigrated.

Would I do it again? Yes. I believe I was right. I believe I defended a basic principle of journalism. It was painful and stressful, but the principles of protecting a source, the right to publish, and the need for law

Imprisonment Without Trial

enforcement to do its own work has never been more evident.

Something else is increasingly evident as well. Prosecutors and police have an awful lot of power to push, cajole and destroy people. Perhaps too much. I've heard rumblings and seen evidence that may indicate that something even more foul has taken place in the Hernandez case.

It is obvious that the prosecutor tried to use me all along for the State's purposes. It's also clear the defense attorneys did the same thing. But in this, I must side with the defense. They're trying to defend a life and the State is trying to take one.

It's sad anytime a police officer dies or anyone dies. But being a police officer or for that matter, President of the United States does not mean you are above the law. Moreover, neither the police nor the prosecution have the right to overreach their authority and destroy all those involved in a case. Thus subverting, instead of guiding justice.

They have tried to do so in the Hernandez case. I wouldn't cooperate; so they tried to destroy my credibility. KMOL wouldn't cooperate; so it cost the station money.

For three years, as of March 27, 1992, Julian and Henry Hernandez have been held in prison in violation of their constitutional right to a speedy trial.

For three years they have been facing capital murder charges despite the revelation of drug use on the night of his death by the police officer involved.

For three years they have faced and still face the possibility they may pay with their lives, even though Julian's involvement seemed minimal and Henry may very well have been fighting for his life.

Why? Because they are poor, Hispanic, and thus

subject to having their rights violated without an outcry.

It's wrong.

And no amount of whitewash can make it right.

Afterword

As I write this, more than three years have come and gone. Henry Hernandez and his brother Julian have not gone to trial for the murder of police officer Gary Williams—not that they ever should. I think the facts show they should both be released. The reasons why I believe this have, I hope, become evident as you read this book.

I am also no longer employed by KMOL TV. The reasons, in my estimation, are similar to those which prompted me to fight for the press's right to protect my sources in the Hernandez case.

I was fired for doing what a reporter is supposed to do—finding out the truth by asking questions. In this juncture, asking President Bush a question regarding the discouraging fight against drugs.

The exchange between President Bush and I which lasted about one minute went something like this:

Karem: How about a local question?
Bush: (pointing in Karem's direction) OK, local ques-

tion to one of these four (presidents). Yes, do you address a question to the Colombian president?

(A reporter standing next to Karem asks Colombian President Cesar Gaviria Trujillo a question, which he answers)

Bush: (pointing to Karem and nodding) This is for one of the three remainders, please.

Karem: Well, actually, it's for you, President Bush. The question I have to ask you, is over the last . . .

Bush: I'm not going to take any more questions, I just told you. You didn't understand it.

Karem: Well, over the last few days . . .

Bush: (gesturing to another reporter) Yes, this lady over here . . .

Karem: Over the last few days, I've . . .

Bush: I'm very sorry, you're dealing with somebody who's made up his mind. And we're trying to be courteous to everybody here. Now if you have a question for one of the other three, ask it. Otherwise, sit down.

Karem: I'd be happy to ask it to one of the other three. I would like for you to answer it as well. I'll ask it to the President of Mexico. Over the . . .

Bush: He's already had a question, sorry.

Karem: He's only had one.

Bush: OK, you go ahead. We're not used to this, but anyway, go ahead.

Karem: Over the . . . Since the Harrison Narcotics Act, the narcotics act, was passed in the United States, God knows when, at the beginning of this century, and since the United States and Mexico have cooperated on drug interdiction efforts countless times since then, I spent some time with narcotics agents over the last few days who made busts who tell us that they're tired. They don't believe the war on drugs can be won. They consider this summit a joke. They consider the presidents cooperating in this summit a joke, as well.

Afterword

What do you tell your people that are fighting it everyday? What do you give them as a morale booster to tell them it's not a joke?
Mexican President Carlos Salinas de Gortari: The most important thing is that there not be any impunity, that those who are drug traffickers in Mexico know that we are going to punish them with the full force that the law allows, with the conviction that by doing so we are protecting our families. Also, by recognizing and being very much aware of the risk they (officers) are undergoing, how many of their lives are at stake. Our effort is totally determined, and we will firmly maintain our efforts with full energy. This is a true war in times of peace that we have decided we will win against drug traffickers.

U.S. News and World Report said, "Brian Karem, some might say got fired for doing his job." Sam Donaldson said at the conclusion of a piece he did for *PrimeTime*, "So, did Brian Karem deserve his fate? Pushy he certainly is, but as Harry Truman said, 'If you can't stand the heat, get out of the kitchen.' Usually, you don't fire the cook."

What's really humorous about all this is that two years ago KMOL, the station at which I worked, spent $100,000 defending my right of free speech. They fired me recently for exercising those very same rights.

Many of the principles originally involved in the Gary Williams/Henry and Julian Hernandez stories are also involved in my new confrontation. So now I must fight on two fronts.

On the first, primarily because of the interview Henry granted me, the State continues to stall. They are appealing a lower court decision that says the interview cannot be used in court.

Meanwhile, I reflect on how the Hernandez interview cost me jail time, personal agony, and became one of the most stressful events in my life. Many ask, was it worth it?

For telling two of the best defense attorneys and the best prosecutors in town to do their own work, Judge Pat Priest sentenced me to six months in jail for contempt of court.

I objected to the utilization of the judicial system to allow some of the best lawyers in town to raid my notebook.

I believe there was a principle involved, buried not too far underneath all the garbage that accumulated as the story snowballed.

First, by keeping a confidential source secret I was again simply doing my job, covering the police beat in San Antonio, Texas, and using every tool a reporter must to inform the public in a timely manner. In fact, my sources were easy enough to find out, had anyone with the power of subpoena decided to do some hard work, instead of grabbing the nearest reporter and shaking him upside down to see what would fall out.

Some have asked me if I am angry I went to jail and others believe I painted myself into a corner that I couldn't get out of, so I had to pretend to do the honorable thing.

I'm not angry at anyone because I went to jail. I'm upset that the system would allow it to happen. And I didn't paint myself into a corner. I knew the consequences of my own actions from day one—true I never thought it would come to jail, but I always knew the possibility existed.

Ironically, a quick review of the facts shows that one page in my reporters note pad contained nothing but three names, some telephone numbers and some crudely drawn doodles. Hardly of earthshaking importance. A federal magistrate said there wasn't anything in those notes either side needed to proceed with his case.

So why, if my sources weren't all that important, and if I had to make such a sacrifice to protect someone, who it turned out in the end didn't understand or appreciate it all that much, why did I do it?

The answer is simple. As reporters, we must exercise our free speech and support a free press. I hope, if for no other reason, my incarceration was important because it gave many people time to pause and reflect on what it is reporters are supposed to do in our business.

Should we be pawns for law enforcement? Should we worry more about our pancake makeup, our appearances, or how we look in a live-shot than on the substance of the real issues we report to the people?

We in the television-news business have been criticized, and rightly so at times, for performing in a shallow medium. The public, it would seem would like us to be more responsible and take our job more seriously.

How, may I ask, are we to perform such a task when the tools we need to do so can be so easily stripped from us?

Good reporters and editors, of course, will not stop gathering information and protecting sources simply because a court of law tells them to.

What some have told me, is that they'll lie when dragged into court. They'll say they've lost their notes or can't remember their source. This was a path available to me which I did not take, nor would I recommend it.

So what's left? Only our own initiative. Lets' challenge the courts to do their own work. We cannot fight every case, but we can put pressure on legislators and politicians whenever possible to keep the press free.

For inspiration in that matter, I turn to H.L. Mencken. Mencken once said he viewed his job as being akin to stirring up the animals in a zoo.

I agree.

It's time to start stirring once again.

This is a photocopy of a page from Brian Karem's notebook, which the KMOL-TV reporter surrendered Tuesday at a hearing seeking his release on contempt of court charges. The three people named each reportedly played a role in facilitating a jailhouse interview with capital murder defendant Henry David Hernandez.

```
KF
8959      Karem, Brian
.P7
K37         Shield the source
1992
```

DUE DATE			
OCT 10 1994			
NOV 21 1994			